Take God to Work

T0168102

COWLEY PUBLICATIONS is a ministry of the brothers of the Society of Saint John the Evangelist, a monastic order in the Episcopal Church. Our mission is to provide books and resources for those seeking spiritual and theological formation. COWLEY PUBLICATIONS is committed to developing a new generation of writers and teachers who will encourage people to think and pray in new ways about spirituality, reconciliation, and the future.

Take God to Work

Gary Moreau

Cowley Publications
CAMBRIDGE, MASSACHUSETTS

Library of Congress Cataloging-in-Publication Data

Moreau, Gary L.
  Take God to work / Gary Moreau.
    p. cm.
  ISBN-10: 1-56101-277-7   ISBN-13: 978-1-56101-277-0
(pbk.: alk. paper) 1. Employees—Religious life. 2. Work—Religious aspects—Christianity. I. Title.
  BV4593.M67 2006
  248.8'8—dc22

                                    2006010411

Cover design: Gary Ragaglia
Interior design: Wendy Holdman

Cowley Publications
4 Brattle Street
Cambridge, Massachusetts 02138
800-225-1534 • www.cowley.org

This book is dedicated to my parents,
Gordon and Patricia Moreau,
who taught me the dignity of all work.

Contents

Take God to Work

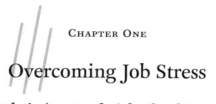

CHAPTER ONE

Overcoming Job Stress

The Christian Yardstick of Achievement

The next time you're driving in rush hour traffic, take a close look at the faces of the drivers around you. Chances are most of them won't look very happy.

Thirty years ago, sociologists predicted that we would work less and relax more in the future. That turned out to be an accurate prediction for most of the industrialized world. In the United States, however, Americans have used much of the 81 percent gain in labor productivity realized between 1970 and 2000 to acquire more wealth, not more leisure time. In fact, according to Harvard economist Juliet B. Schor, author of *The Overworked American*, employed Americans are on the job an additional 163 hours per year today than they were in 1969.

Most of us live in a nicer house or apartment and have more financial security than our parents did at the same age. While we've acquired a lot of stuff, however, consumerism hasn't provided many of us with more

3

fulfilling, less stressful lives. The Conference Board's annual survey of American households in 2002 found that almost one in two American adults (49 percent) is unhappy in his or her current job, up from 41 percent in 1995.

How many people do you know whose jobs are interfering with their personal relationships? What about you? Is your job more stressful than it used to be? Do you have more work than you can handle? How many people have you encountered lately who say that they are considering quitting their job?

It would be easy to attribute this to the tragic events of 9/11 and its tumultuous aftermath. However, while world events have challenged each of us to look deep within ourselves, our collective workplace malaise is not so simply explained.

What is at the heart of all this workplace stress and how can we reduce it? For the answer, consider the story of Joseph, as told in the book of Genesis.

Who's in Control?

Joseph was the son of Jacob and Rachel, Jacob's favorite wife. Though Rachel's firstborn, Joseph was the eleventh son of Jacob and would ultimately go on to father one of the twelve tribes of Israel. Before doing so, however, he had more than his fair share of trials and tribulations.

For starters, Joseph's older half-brothers despised him. He was clearly Jacob's favorite and had, perhaps imprudently, shared a dream that suggested his superiority over them. Needless to say, they were pretty jealous of the attention lauded on Joseph and put off by Joseph's perceived arrogance. Ultimately, they plotted to get Joseph out of the picture.

They sold Joseph to a caravan of Ishmaelite merchants who, in turn, took him to Egypt and sold him to Potiphar, one of Pharaoh's officials. Despite his misfortune, however, Joseph was loyal and hard-working, and Potiphar rewarded him with ever-increasing responsibility, eventually putting him in charge of the entire household. Things were looking up for Joseph.

Potiphar's wife, however, was greatly attracted to the handsome Joseph and schemed to get him into her bed. The pious Joseph refused, but the jilted wife told Potiphar that Joseph had tried to rape her—and she had his cloak, which she had ripped off him when he ran from the house, to back her claim.

Potiphar, of course, wasn't happy and threw Joseph in prison. While some biblical scholars suggest that Potiphar may have doubted his wife's story, since the punishment for the attempted rape of the wife of a high

Egyptian official was typically death, it was yet another setback in Joseph's stressful existence. If being enslaved weren't bad enough, he was now imprisoned.

Nonetheless, Joseph once again made the best of the situation and ultimately gained the trust and respect of the warden. In fact, the warden was so impressed that he put Joseph in charge of the prisoners.

How many people, do you suppose, would have maintained a positive attitude after being sold into slavery and then imprisoned over a false accusation? Most of us wouldn't be whistling while we worked after all that. We'd be pretty stressed out, to say the least. Joseph, however, didn't use his misfortunes to rationalize defiance or laziness. He didn't plot to cheat or ruin his masters. He remained trustworthy and hard-working through it all.

How could Joseph maintain such an attitude in the face of such stress and adversity? The answer lies in Joseph's unwavering faith in God, who continued to watch over Joseph no matter what the circumstances were. Joseph's faith gave him a purpose and hope for the future. In fact, Joseph had *only* purpose. He had no money. He had no power. He had no title or fancy office. He didn't even have his freedom. Yet he knew in his heart that God was preparing him for something. And indeed God was. Joseph's faith gave him something that no one could take away from him. It was something that he could control, even in an uncontrollable situation.

Job titles, earnings, and possessions are all things that can be taken away. They are external to who we really are. When we measure our lives by these external standards, we give control over to someone else. And that's where stress comes into the picture.

Writing in *Personnel Today*, Simon Kent describes stress as "a combination of anxiety, frustration and sometimes anger *at the perceived lack of control* [emphasis added] they [workers] have over their circumstances." In other words, it's not pressure, or workload, or even uncertainty that is at the heart of workplace stress. It's the issue of control—or the lack thereof.

According to the National Institute for Occupational Safety and Health, "The concept of job stress is often confused with challenge, but these concepts are not the same." Challenge energizes us. Stress is debilitating and often results from "hectic and routine tasks that have little inherent meaning . . . and provide little sense of control."

In other words, stress is not a result of responsibility or workload. Think, for example, of the tremendous responsibility pilots or air traffic controllers have. However, if they are comfortable that they are working within their capabilities, their training, and their equipment, they may feel little stress. It's not unlike great athletes who do incredible things in the heat of a contest if they can play "within themselves." Challenge is an enabler as long as people believe it is within their capability.

Capability, appropriately, starts with the letter "c," the first letter in the word "control." However, what we are capable of, when it comes to work, is not always in our control. Few of us, in fact, have unilateral control over our areas of responsibility. Ironically, most workers have more control over what they can *prevent* from happening than what they can accomplish. A store clerk with a bad attitude can drive customers away. Even the most professional store clerks, however, can only sell products that the customers want at a price that customers are willing to pay. Despite legend to the contrary, I've never actually seen anyone sell ice to penguins.

While it is true that hard work and perseverance often pay off in improved results, there are no guarantees. In fact, there is often little more than a casual relationship between hard work and success in the workplace. Employees in troubled companies frequently say they work harder after the company is in trouble than they ever did when it was prospering.

What about you? When things aren't going well in your job, do you go home early or take time off to play a little golf? I doubt it. If you're like me, you burn the midnight oil trying to get things back on track. You buckle down and double your efforts.

Think about the things your boss expects from you. How many are actually within your control? How many of those expectations can you accomplish entirely on your own, regardless of what anyone else does, or what happens in whatever marketplace you serve?

That doesn't mean that your hard work and dedication won't lead to achievements. It is to say, however, that the achievement of these goals will not be entirely up to you. You may be thinking, "If I can't control these things anyway, why not just do my best and hope that a little luck will come my way? If it doesn't, at least I'll have done my best."

That's a good attitude—in theory. In practice, however, it misses the point. It assumes that achievement will bring you fulfillment and eliminate your stress. It won't.

For starters, workplace achievement often leads to more responsibility, more challenge, and more pressure to perform. The bottom line is, workplace achievement doesn't eliminate stress. The underlying reason is that even realized achievement is not fully in our control. And if we can't fully control the things that lead to achievement, we can't fully prevent losing the spoils of achievement.

What is it that you want from your work? A raise?

A big bonus? A promotion? A pat on the back? The respect of your peers? A corner office? Whatever it is, chances are that it is largely external to your personal sphere of control. And whatever you achieve can always be taken away. In the end, you borrow your achievements. You can never own them. If you measure your personal worth by the external yardsticks of your title, your earnings, the number of people you supervise, or the assets in your care, you are putting that worth and identity in the hands of others.

There are some things, however, that can never be taken away. Consider the story of Martha and Mary from the book of Luke.

A Lesson in Faith

Traveling with his disciples, Jesus came to the home of two sisters, Martha and Mary. They could not have been more different. While Martha fretted and scurried about making preparations for their visitors, Mary sat at the feet of Jesus and listened to what he had to say.

Frustrated by her sister's lack of help, Martha finally asked Jesus to tell Mary to stop loafing and get to work. Jesus, however, refused, scolding Martha for being so uptight about such inconsequential matters.

Mary, he noted, had the right priorities. His message was what really mattered.

Does Martha's complaint sound familiar? It is, perhaps, the most common complaint heard in the workplace today: "So and so is not pulling her weight." "He's a slacker." "I have to do everything myself."

Martha was not a bad person. After all, she had opened up her home to Jesus and obviously went to some effort to ensure that he had a pleasant and comfortable stay.

Nor does it appear that Jesus was unappreciative of Martha's effort. He didn't suggest that the chores should be ignored or that the house should be allowed to decay into ruin.

This is, nonetheless, clearly a story about priorities. Mary chose faith, while Martha worried and was anxious about all of those things that occupy our days.

As in the story of Joseph, there is a critical distinction between achievement and faith. Achievement is an external standard that can be taken away as quickly as Joseph lost his standing in Potiphar's house. Mary's internal commitment to faith, by contrast, "will not be taken away from her" (Luke 10:42).

That doesn't mean that we shouldn't take pride in our workplace achievements, or that our pride in doing something well won't bring some sense of satisfaction.

Pride, however, is a backward-looking emotion. The achievement on which our pride is built is behind us. It's a "done deal." Fulfillment, which is what each of us yearns for, requires a sense of taking something into the future.

Ultimately, that is the difference between achievement and faith. Achievement is an assessment of the past. Faith represents hope for the future. Achievement is static. Faith is vibrant and alive.

It might be easy to assume that faith is a gift that keeps growing all by itself. However, Mary's example gives us a clue about our part in that process: She "sat at the Lord's feet listening to what he said" (Luke 10:39). She was learning. She was actively participating in her faith through her acquisition of knowledge.

I am reminded of something my father used to ask when he put my sister and brother and me to bed at night. He always wanted to know what we had learned that day. Whatever our answer, he would say, "A day without learning is a wasted day."

Knowledge, like faith, is something no one can take away from us. It is forever ours. To acquire knowledge we have to be open to it. We need to listen to what people say to us. We need to see the world around us. We need to be perpetual students of life. It's not enough just to do. We must do and *learn*, do and *absorb*, do and *appreciate*.

And knowledge, like faith, can't just be filed away and forgotten about. We need to exercise it, just as we need to exercise a muscle or practice a skill. Even memories need to be dusted off periodically and exposed to conscious thought. As new knowledge is acquired, we have to take the time to appreciate how it relates to the knowledge we've acquired in the past. Just as faith is a continual work-in-process that requires our constant attention, so, too, does our knowledge require ongoing care and nurturing. Just as the benefits of faith go well beyond the faith itself, the benefits of knowledge and learning go well beyond their mere acquisition.

I once worked with a salesperson who was well past the normal retirement age. He had been quite successful and didn't appear to be in need of income. He clearly loved his work, however, and his customers, without exception, adored and respected him. He was, in everyone's assessment, the best of the best.

This fellow did not have the personality traits that you would normally associate with being a successful salesman. He wasn't tall or particularly good-looking. He didn't walk around with a perpetual smile on his face. He didn't appear to be particularly outgoing. And I don't recall him ever telling a joke or a humorous story.

I once asked a co-worker who had worked with

him for many years what he believed was the key to this salesman's success. Without the slightest hesitation, the co-worker explained that the salesman was completely committed to self-improvement. Each and every day this individual undertook some learning process, little of which had anything to do with being a better salesman *per se.* He simply wanted to be a better person, and he believed that the constant acquisition of knowledge was the key.

In this case, this man's internal standard of learning also led to professional success by the external standards of his trade. But the true measure of his success was his motivation. If our commitment to internal standards is motivated solely by our expectation of externally measured success, our motivation is insincere. God is never fooled by appearances because appearances are external to who we really are. Appearances are for others. God, however, always knows the truth that lies within.

Consider the story from the book of Mark about the wealthy man who came to Jesus.

A Lesson in Priorities

Traveling through the region of Judea, Jesus was approached by a rich young man who had lived his life by the Ten Commandments. When he asked Jesus what he needed to do to enter heaven, however, Jesus told him to sell all of his possessions and give the money to the poor. The man, Jesus knew, was greatly attached to his wealth, and the directive filled the young man with despair.

As with the Mary and Martha story, this is a lesson in priorities. It is also a lesson in sincerity. And it's one of many times throughout the Bible where we're told that *how* we live is more important than how we *don't*. The fact that this rich man did *not* violate the commandments was outweighed by the fact that he *did* worship his wealth, since the thought of its loss saddened him greatly.

To put it another way, while our internal standards define us, our external standards define the true nature of those internal standards. They are not mutually exclusive. Jesus did not say that the wealthy could not have sincere faith. But if wealth is what they truly live for, there can be no real faith.

Our external standards of success are idols of our own making. As Mother Teresa wrote, "God has not created poverty; it is we who have created it. Before God, all of us are poor." Wealth and poverty have not been defined by God. There were no titles or corner offices or stock options in the Garden of Eden.

When we measure ourselves against external standards of wealth, power, or beauty, we can never realize ultimate achievement. Such achievements are relative. Someone more "accomplished" will always come along. There will always be someone who is prettier or more handsome, who is smarter, a better athlete, or has accumulated more wealth. Athletic achievements don't go unbroken forever. Fortunes come and go. Most of the richest people in the world today probably won't be a generation from now. Not even the most beautiful Hollywood starlet or handsome leading man can completely escape the effects of aging. "The best" and "the most" are fleeting standards staked in shifting sands.

When I was a young boy, I played Pop Warner football. There was a maximum weight limit at the time of 115 pounds, and I weighed in at 114.75. Not surprisingly, the coach made me a lineman. And I was pretty good. I started on both offense and defense, and I got my share of accolades in the local newspaper (e.g., "Moreau anchored the defensive line throughout the game").

The following year I went out for the freshman football team. I went into the first practice confident that I would be a starter and already dreaming of my inevitable glory as a gridiron star. I was again assigned to the linemen squad, although this time it wasn't a function of my size. I was simply too slow to play any other position.

And, unfortunately, I wasn't much bigger than I

had been a year before. I might have ballooned up to 120 pounds at most. So the first time I actually had to block someone in practice, I found myself facing a very strong, fit, young farm boy who easily outweighed me by 100 pounds. Needless to say, the whistle blew, and I was flat on my back before I knew it. Within a week I had transferred to the soccer team, and my glory days of football were over. I had to find a new yardstick of achievement.

In the extreme, external standards of value and achievement are the fuel of envy, the most destructive emotion of all. It is impossible to find happiness or fulfillment if we live under its yoke.

Faith, on the other hand, is the internal yardstick by which all other things are measured. The most powerful person on earth is powerless compared to God. As the Creator of beauty and athleticism, intelligence and imagination, God certainly has no need for money. What God does want, however, is our faith.

If you are one of those unfulfilled faces that peer blankly through the windshield on the way home each night, or if you feel overwhelmed by the stress of your job, it will do you little good to blame your boss or your employer or your circumstances. Instead, re-evaluate the yardstick by which you measure achievement in your job and the purposes you seek to achieve.

Chances are that you are judging yourself and your work by external standards of value and merit over which you have less influence than you may like to believe. *The resulting lack of control is at the heart of your stress.*

All of God's standards are internal. When you choose to pursue a relationship with God, and value the faith that accompanies the journey, you will have something that no one can deny you or ultimately take away. Only then will you have control over the stress in your life.

Chapter Two

Overcoming Loneliness and Isolation

Christian Sincerity

Do you ever feel invisible at work? Unappreciated? Unaccepted? Alone?

We often feel the most isolated in a large group. It's easy to live in a large city and suffer constant loneliness. Or to sit in an audience and feel like just a face in the crowd. In the workplace, the sense of loneliness and isolation can be greatly exacerbated when everyone is busy and under pressure, when there's too much to do and too little time in which to do it. It's easy to treat each other with indifference and apathy when our plate is full.

Moreover, the workplace environment promotes individualism over belonging. While there may be a lot of talk about teamwork, or even family, the recognition and reward systems—other than the occasional certificate of appreciation given to small-project teams—focus on the individual employee. Most work environments are designed to promote competition, not connection.

In short, the workplace is a fabricated social environment where the fear that others will take advantage of us at the first possible opportunity creates isolation.

I believe that employers and employees instinctively realize this. That is why so much time and money is spent attempting to rally enthusiasm and spirit at many companies. Most employers recognize that the workplace is fundamentally impersonal and uninspiring.

There's nothing wrong with trying to generate company spirit *per se*. More often than not, however, these efforts are misdirected. The willingness to work hard and the desire to succeed are typically not the problems afflicting most workplaces. What's lacking is a sense of belonging that transcends self-interest.

We all have a deep-seated need for connection to the people and the world around us. Even the lone wolves among us want to be part of something bigger than ourselves. "Winning" doesn't fulfill that need. We can be proud of our accomplishments and still wonder how those accomplishments give our lives meaning and purpose. In the end, they really don't.

There have been scores of professional athletes and Hollywood stars who have suffered tremendous emotional pain despite their success and celebrity. Consider what Judy Garland, one of the most famous actresses of all time, had to say on the subject: "If I'm such a legend, then why am I so lonely? Let me tell you, legends are all very well if you've got somebody around you who loves you."

Belonging, not accomplishment, is the key to personal fulfillment. Belonging is a state of being; an accomplishment is a short-term event, a result at a point of time. Accomplishment may bring material rewards, but it doesn't satisfy the personal need for human connection. As Mother Theresa once wrote, "Loneliness, and the feeling of being unwanted, is the most terrible poverty."

Created for Connection

As a child, you probably learned the story of Adam and Eve from the book of Genesis. Whatever theological meaning you read into the Genesis account about men and women, and the relationship between the two, the core message is clear: God instilled in us the need for companionship. We are social creatures with a deep yearning for connection. We were created to belong.

Belonging gives us identity and purpose. We all need to be associated with something, to be recognized as a member of a group with some common linkage. Think about how you define yourself. Chances are that you identify yourself through your connections. Some of those connections are with people whom you are naturally related to, such as your family or people born in the same country. Others are connections of choice, and it is these voluntary connections that collectively define who you are.

Ultimately, our personal identity is fundamentally linked to a group identity. Even if we claim to be unique, we can only be unique in a group context. If we fancy ourselves to be the prettiest or most handsome person in town, for example, we are identifying ourselves through those people who value beauty. Even if we define ourselves by our independence and free spirit, our personal worth is validated only to the extent that others value these things. In the end we all need approval from someone. In a very real sense, self-worth is the reflection we see in the mirrored faces of others. We are who we are only on a relative basis; we are who we are only through others. Identity cannot be achieved in isolation.

There are, of course, certain facts that distinguish us from the people around us, such as our height, weight, and hair color. Seldom, however, are these the traits that we want to be known for. They're superficial and impersonal. Even the most beautiful women and the most handsome men want to be thought of as more than a pretty face.

Our physical presence, similarly, is not sufficient for us to have a sense of belonging. It's possible to stand in the middle of a crowd, and feel very isolated and alone. Or to work in a sea of cubicles, and feel cloistered and forsaken. Belonging requires a sense of connection.

At the age of nineteen, I took a leave of absence from college to travel the country and work through the grief of having recently lost my father. It was in the early seventies, and the economy was in very rough shape. Unemployment was very high, and many men and women, young and old alike, were forced to leave their homes and families to find work elsewhere.

I eventually ended up in the Colorado mountains where there was a large construction project involving a big mine and smelter and all of the infrastructure that goes along with them. Men had come from all over the country looking for work.

The most menial jobs, which were all I was qualified for, were awarded at the beginning of each day. Early every morning, I would stand with a large group of other men looking for work, our work gloves and lunch pails in hand, in front of the hiring office. At the beginning of the shift, a man would emerge and announce how many workers were needed that day. He would then visually scan the crowd and point to the few men he wanted. They would climb onto a waiting truck, and the rest of us would go home and hope for better luck the next day.

Talk about *not* belonging. They didn't even want to know our names. We were a faceless herd of bodies for hire. I was surrounded by people, yet I felt only the superficial connection of our shared unemployment with any of them.

My isolation, however, was not a function of the people around me. It was a function of the demeaning and impersonal circumstances. But even when we're surrounded by great co-workers, if we aren't treated with respect and dignity, we will feel a sense of debilitating isolation.

Psychologist Abraham Maslow (1908–1970) recognized the importance of belonging in his now-famous "hierarchy of needs," published in 1943. In simple terms, he believed that human needs fall into five hierarchical categories, and that each need can be satisfied only when all the needs that precede it have been satisfied. In ascending order, those five levels of need are:

- Physiological Needs
- Safety Needs
- Love & Belonging Needs
- Esteem Needs
- Self-Actualization

To reach the top of the hierarchy, to self-actualize, is to reach one's full potential. Taken in its broadest sense, it is what each of us ultimately strives for. It is the personal fulfillment that makes us "whole," gives us a sense of life purpose, and provides meaning to our existence.

We must start this journey by first satisfying our physiological needs for food, water, sleep, warmth—all of the needs of basic human existence. These, as Maslow identifies, are needs that simply can't be ignored. If we fail to satisfy them, we will cease to exist.

Having met our physiological needs, we must then satisfy our need for safety. No one wants to live in constant fear. And, unfortunately, if we ignore our basic need for safety, danger will inevitably knock at our door. We can't simply opt out of life's aggressive side.

Once we are physiologically satisfied and safe, the need we must satisfy next is that of belonging. We must find a group to be part of. Whatever ties our "group" together, we must join in before we can hope to find personal fulfillment. This need to belong is an extraordinarily well-understood but often overlooked reality. Figuratively speaking, belonging is what makes the world go round.

Maslow considered the need to belong so fundamental and so great that he referred to it as an "instinctoid": an instinct-like need similar to the instinctive need to breathe. Belonging, in other words, is not optional.

In fact, as Maslow's hierarchy suggests, we cannot

achieve esteem until we belong. Esteem, at every level, requires the participation of others because esteem includes not only self-esteem but the respect we get from others. That is why belonging and connection are so critical to personal fulfillment. We all need validation. We all need reassurance. We all need to know that we are valuable to someone.

Another reason belonging is so important is that we live in a frightening world. No one knows what tomorrow will bring. In belonging, we acquire a sense of security that we will not have to face it alone. This is where faith becomes critical to the hierarchy of needs. Consider the story in Luke of one woman's faith.

Secure in Love

The story recounts a dinner Jesus had at one of the Pharisee's homes. A local woman with a very bad reputation showed up and began to wash the feet of Jesus "with her tears." As if that weren't enough, she wiped his feet "with her hair, kissed them and poured perfume on them" (Luke 7:38)!

The host, who was familiar with the sinful life the woman had lived, was appalled, even incredulous, that Jesus would allow such a person to touch him. In response Jesus, as he often did, told the Pharisee a story.

It involved a moneylender who had forgiven the debts of two men incapable of repaying him. One man, however, owed ten times as much money as the other man, making the former even more appreciative of the forgiveness than the latter.

The sinful woman, of course, was analogous to the man with the greater debt. But because she had shown such extraordinary love toward Jesus, her equally extraordinary sins were forgiven. It didn't matter what she had done in the past. It mattered only that she loved Jesus and had faith in him. Through her faith, she found connection and recognition and knew the love of God.

The wonderful news for all of us is that God recognizes everyone who has faith. Always! There are no exceptions. It matters not how others of this world treat us. It matters not what title we have or how much importance others attribute to us. It matters not what wealth or social status has been bestowed upon us. Each of us can find connection through faith. Each of us can belong.

Through faith, we come to know the unrestrained and limitless love of God. And with that love, and through that love, we can satisfy our need for belonging. Most groups that we belong to are transient and tentative. Their bonds can be washed away by the natural ebb and flow of life. Even the family, which is the most likely to be sustained, is not permanent. God's love, on the other hand, is invulnerable and eternal. No outside force can weaken its bond. Not even time can erode its strength. This is why, as poet Antoine de Saint-Exupéry observed, "Loneliness is bred of a mind that has grown earth-bound." Only God's love can give us an eternal sense of belonging.

No other form of security comes close to the sanctuary of God's love. To put it in perspective, consider a passage from the book of Romans:

> Who shall separate us from the love of Christ? Shall trouble or hardship or persecution or famine or nakedness or danger or sword? As it is written: "For your sake we face death all day long; we are considered as sheep to be slaughtered."
>
> No, in all these things we are more than conquerors through him who loved us. For I am convinced that neither death nor life, neither angels nor demons, neither the present nor the future, nor any powers, neither height nor depth, nor anything else in all creation, will be able to separate us from the love of God that is in Christ Jesus our Lord.
>
> ROMANS 8:35–39

How can we ever be lonely knowing that God is on our side? How can any of us feel isolated and marginalized knowing that nothing of this world or any other can separate us from God's love? Can there be any greater sense of belonging? Can there be any greater source of hope and security?

But the good news doesn't stop there. Our relationship with God lays the groundwork for our relationships with each other. Knowing we are loved enables us to reach out to others, which, in turn, motivates them to reach out to us. By satisfying their need to belong, we satisfy our own. Said differently, belonging is first and foremost up to us, not them. We must take the first step. As Dale Carnegie once said, "You can make more friends in two months by becoming interested in other people than you can in two years by trying to get other people interested in you."

If you think about the people you feel the closest to, they're probably people whom you've reached out to in the past. They are the people who will go the extra mile for you because they know you will do the same for them.

About seven years ago, my wife and I moved into a new subdivision. We didn't know any of our neighbors. Nor did any of them know each other. Today, however, it is a very close community, and although

I could live anywhere and still pursue my writing, we have chosen to stay. The reason is simple: We belong.

How did that happen? Personal compatibility, of course, is part of it. But that doesn't explain it all. I've lived in other neighborhoods where there was personal compatibility and never achieved the same sense of belonging.

The difference here is that people give to each other. When my neighbor had surgery a couple of years back, I mowed his lawn for the next four weeks. He didn't ask me to. He pleaded, in fact, to let him hire a lawn service.

The following winter, my wife and I were out of town when a big snowstorm hit. When we arrived home, we discovered that another neighbor had shoveled our driveway. The woman who had agreed to watch our cat had put a gallon of milk, a loaf of bread, and a dozen eggs in the refrigerator for our return.

In actuality, our neighborhood is pretty diverse. We belong to different churches and pursue our faith in different ways. Yet through God's love, and through giving of ourselves, we connect with each other.

In the end, God's love is the key to belonging. Connection with those around us is a mirror of our connection to God.

Sincerity at the Source

On the surface, many workplaces try to foster connection. There may be office parties, company sports teams, corporate-sponsored projects or events. Many managers instinctively appreciate the need to establish some sense of connection with the people they supervise. And there are thousands of management books to tell them how, with prescriptions ranging from eating lunch in the employee cafeteria to stripping out the visible signs of hierarchy, such as ties and personal offices.

These are not bad ideas *per se*. But no matter how good the technique is, without sincerity, there can be no connection. Without sincerity, we can never be fully accepted. As Ralph Waldo Emerson once wrote, "A friend is a person with whom I may be sincere. Before him I may think aloud."

Too often we try to convince people of our sincerity with only our words. However, it is common but frequently ignored wisdom that people respond to what we *do*, not what we *say*. In the workplace, more often than not, that means people respond to what is *in*-spected, not what is *ex*-pected. If you, as a manager, for example, tell your employees that the door is always open for them, but you're always too busy to be interrupted, your words, however sincere, have no meaning. By the same token, if you tell the boss only what you think he or she wants to hear, or to offer complimentary remarks or gestures only to "butter up" the boss, your words are empty.

Sincerity is the universal element of connection, but it is also an entirely personal attribute. The latest bestseller on leadership or career success may prescribe a style that is extremely effective for *an* individual— usually the one who wrote the book. Often, however, it is a style ill-suited to everyone. Efforts to implement someone else's style will only come across as insincere— and will be ineffective.

To be sincere is to be honest, frank, and respectful. Sincerity is freedom from arrogance or deceit. It is the surrender of superiority. It is to interface with others in a humble manner. French author Henri Peyre wrote, "The primary condition for being sincere is the same as for being humble: not to boast of it, and probably not even to be aware of it."

The Bible constantly reminds us of the importance of humility. Consider what the Apostle Peter had to say.

The Importance of Humility

In an open letter to Christians who were facing a time of intense persecution and isolation within the Roman Empire, Peter wrote:

To the elders among you, I appeal as a fellow elder, a witness of Christ's sufferings and one who also will share in the glory to be revealed: Be shepherds of God's flock that is under your care, serving as overseers—not because you must, but because you are willing, as God wants you to be; not greedy for money, but eager to serve; not lording it over those entrusted to you, but being examples to the flock. And when the Chief Shepherd appears, you will receive the crown of glory that will never fade away.

Young men, in the same way be submissive to those who are older. All of you, clothe yourselves with humility toward one another, because, "God opposes the proud but gives grace to the humble."

Humble yourselves, therefore, under God's mighty hand, that he may lift you up in due time.

1 PETER 5:1-6

This passage is particularly relevant to the modern workplace, for it acknowledges the natural social order of life. While not unique to the workplace or to modern times, the modern workplace has formalized the "pecking order" or the steps up the corporate ladder. How would you describe your own boss? Does he or she "lord it" over you? You may or may not be able to change that attitude. Nonetheless, this passage to the elders does have immediate personal relevance: It reinforces the importance of humility. Isn't Peter ultimately telling the elders that they must, above all else, be humble and sincere?

Peter goes even further, telling the young Christians to treat *each other* with humility: "God opposes the proud, but gives grace to the humble."

But is that how it works in your workplace? Does your boss applaud humility or are you more likely to get recognition for self-promotion? Have you ever heard of anyone in your workplace lauded as a humble go-getter?

There are two primary reasons for the apparent diminution of humility in the modern workplace. The first has to do with the mutation of authority into power. The second has to do with a common lack of understanding of the meaning and role of sincerity.

Authority is a technical right. Executives have the authority to sign checks or to enter into contracts on behalf of the company. Your boss has the authority to sign off on your performance review, approve your expense reports, and evaluate your eligibility for promotions. That authority can be leveraged into the power to influence behavior. If we know that someone has the authority to influence our future, we are naturally responsive to that person's expectations, even expectations that are only marginally related to the tasks at hand. The resulting accommodation can be as minor as how we dress or communicate, or as severe as co-operating in immoral or illegal activities.

In the end, however, while the people we work for may have authority that we can do little about, they can leverage that authority into power only to the extent we allow them to. No one can force us to be anyone that we are not or to do anything that we are unwilling to do.

To the extent that we feel that we have no choice, we are merely surrendering to the impersonal value system of job title, status, and income. But the truth is, we always have a choice. Choice, when it comes to the things that matter, cannot be taken away. It must be surrendered.

This is where the misunderstanding of sincerity, and its inward counterpart, humility, comes into play. Sincerity and humility are not symbolic realities. You can't appear to be humble. You must *be* humble.

Humility in Action

In the competitive, results-oriented workplace, we tend to react to humility with skepticism because it is sometimes falsely used for advantage. In an "everyone for themselves" environment, we're understandably skeptical of the humble, the self-less.

I once went to work in a new office where the receptionist was extremely outgoing and friendly. At first, I admit, I was a little skeptical. Over time, however, the woman's sincerity bore through my wall of cynicism until I accepted that her excessive concern for everyone around her was genuine.

Feeling guilty, and more than a little curious, I began to speak with her at greater length. I discovered that she had led an extremely difficult life. She had endured an abusive husband, a drug-addicted daughter, and extreme financial hardship. She got through it, she explained, through her faith, and, through faith, dropping all pretenses toward others. The circumstances of her life forced humility upon her, and she chose to turn that humility into strength.

All too often we think of humility as surrender or concession. Humility, many mistakenly believe, is an admission of failure or inferiority. That perspective, however, reflects a value system defined by competition and accomplishment, in which victory is a feat rather than a state of mind. Instead of being a weakness that calls for concessions, humility is a strength that creates connections.

It is important, however, not to confuse humility

with valuing yourself by what others think. If you allow others to define you, you are severing the connection to your self. True humility allows you to connect with your deepest self, and therefore with others at a more intimate level.

So the next time you're feeling isolated and alone among your fellow workers, don't respond by fortifying your defenses, or by trying to say or do something that is falsely humble or insincere. The former will only sever you from them, while the latter will only serve to sever them from you.

Instead, invigorate your faith—and the sincerity and humility that faith both requires and allows. Faith is the ultimate protection against loneliness and isolation. With faith, you will know the strength of God's love, which, in turn, will allow you to belong. Faith in God is the only sure and lasting remedy for loneliness and isolation.

Chapter Three

Recognition and Reward

Christian Perspective

Is your boss fair in handing out assignments, rewards, and recognition?

American society was literally built around the idea of fairness. The founding fathers of the United States believed that freedom—the political form of fairness— is an inalienable right and that the equality on which it depends is a self-evident truth.

The free-market capitalism on which the U.S. economy is based is similarly built around the idea of fairness. In theory, what economists call "efficient markets" give every participant in every commercial transaction equal opportunity. When knowledgeable consumers exercise free choice, and manufacturers and service providers are allowed to compete for their business on equal terms, the fundamental tenet of American capitalism is that the optimal, or *fairest*, result is achieved.

The American workplace, as economists view it, is just another market, like the market for tomatoes or automobiles. In this case, however, it is the skill and effort of individuals that are being traded, putting a practical and ideological premium on the need for fairness.

American employers, for the most part, have attempted to create a fair workplace where competition among employees for advancement, reward, and recognition is supposed to give the employer the best possible workforce performance while affording each worker an equal opportunity to be rewarded and recognized. But is that how it happens at your company?

Most workplace organizations have a pyramid structure that rewards workers as they move up toward the top. If it's a young organization, there may still be hope among all employees that they will be the ones to make it to the top, but there will inevitably be fewer opportunities than candidates. Most of us accept that we can't all be the CEO. There are, however, other key factors that get in the way of recognition.

Who Gets the Credit?

The first roadblock to recognition has to do with communication. It is a fact that the hierarchy of authority leads to a hierarchy of communication. Imagine the classic ancient battle scene where a long line of soldiers is waiting for the order to attack. That order comes from some person of authority in the back who can't possibly communicate directly with each soldier in the long line, so the command is passed along through the ranks. It's much the same in many organizations. The ultimate decision-maker communicates with a manageable number of senior officers, who in turn communicate with a manageable number of junior officers, and so on and so on, until the order reaches the front line in a relatively timely and consistent manner.

Theoretically, communication in reverse works the same way. Workers at the bottom of the pyramid—who are often the ones with the most direct contact with the customers or the process of providing whatever product or service the company is in business to provide—are asked to give their managers timely, unfiltered information. Frequently, however, information doesn't move up the organization as efficiently as it moves down. Sometimes, by the time information gets to the top, it barely resembles the original information and/or its origin is unclear.

I have found this to be particularly true where competitors are involved, and somebody has to deliver bad news. People naturally associate the message, good or bad, with the person delivering it.

But the problem goes deeper than "shooting the messenger." In trying to overcome the inevitable hurdles that face them, companies often become truth averse. They actively attempt to nurture a "can do" culture that doesn't make excuses. The difference between an explanation and an excuse, however, is often one of perspective. And where different levels of authority are involved, and individuals are in direct competition with each other for recognition and reward, it's just too easy to confuse the former and the latter.

If there has been a big success in your department, who delivers the news to your boss's boss? In most cases, it's your boss. This, of course, creates an opportunity for your boss to take credit for your accomplishments. It happens every day. There's a lot at stake, and it's easy to do.

There doesn't have to be malicious intent for upward communication to get distorted. Truly malicious distortion is the exception rather than the norm. Most people are just trying to do their jobs to the best of their ability. Even where there is no malicious intent, however, your boss may still get credit for your successes simply because he or she is the messenger. Regardless of his or her contribution, your boss is the one with the face time.

Just doing a good job sometimes isn't enough. I believe people understand this instinctively, which is one of the reasons why there is so much political maneuvering in many workplaces. Workers know that there are serious flaws in the communication process that lead to flaws in the recognition process.

What Do You Expect?

There is another theorem of organizational behavior that can escalate communication problems. It's a variation of what psychologists call "precognitive conclusion," which essentially means that we all see what we expect to see. Some scientists believe that the human brain processes as little as one-billionth of the information available to it before reaching a conclusion. It's a matter of efficiency. If our brains processed all of the information available, we wouldn't get much done in a day.

Precognitive conclusion is the reason magicians can trick us with their slight of hand. It's also why we sometimes don't immediately notice that a friend has shaved off his mustache or changed her hair style. In the workplace, precognitive conclusion causes us to attribute success to those we think most highly of to begin with. If the boss thinks that Joe is a superstar, the boss is likely to give Joe the credit for department successes—especially where individual contribution is difficult to determine. If the boss thinks Mary is a poor performer, on the other hand, the boss will be slow to recognize her achievements and quick to recognize her failures.

We do the same thing in our personal lives. If one of our children is mischievous, for example, we're likely to think of that child when we discover the aftermath of mischief.

It's a vicious cycle. As with distorted communication, it's not necessarily malicious. It's just the way things work, even if it's not fair.

Did you ever see the movie *The Usual Suspects*? Every workplace has them. They're the people everyone assumes had something to do with the organization's failings.

Suspicion is just a negative form of expectation, and it permeates our society, particularly the workplace. Just ask the convicted felon who has paid his or her time, genuinely reformed, and is now looking for a job. Just ask the job applicant whose former boss shares unfounded accusations of inappropriate behavior with prospective employers who call for a reference.

It works the other way, too. If the boss doesn't expect you to be a top performer, he or she is unlikely to give you the credit you deserve when you solve a difficult problem or achieve a challenging goal.

Do you remember the childhood story of the tortoise and the hare? Like most childhood stories, it's firmly planted in reality. It is the hares who typically get all the attention. Sometimes, however, it is the tortoise who wins the race.

I can think of many examples from my own career. One, however, is particularly memorable. It involves a salesman who was, in many respects, the least flashy in the entire sales force. He was quiet and unassuming and often disheveled in appearance. He didn't stand up at sales meetings to share tales of his conquests. The sales in his territory, in fact, were relatively low when compared to the rest of the country.

He was, however, the hardest worker in the entire division. Even at the age of sixty, he got down on his hands and knees in the stores and made sure that the displays of our products were clean and tidy and well-positioned. His customers loved him, and, as we would eventually discover, he had a very challenging territory. His sales, while not that high when compared to other territories, were double what any other salesperson could achieve under the same circumstances.

How Do You Measure Success?

The problem of giving fair recognition is compounded by the fallacy that personal performance in the workplace can be objectively measured and evaluated. It can't.

Every place of employment likes to think of itself as a meritocracy where employees are recognized and rewarded on the basis of their personal performance. But, as Dr. Richard H.G. Field, Professor of Strategic Management and Organization at the University of Alberta, wrote, that assumes "that performance is a knowable and observable objective reality and that performance ratings are reasonable reflections of that reality." Because of things like pyramid communication and precognitive conclusion, on top of the complexity behind most workplace success and failure and a lack of firsthand observation, that is seldom the case.

Researchers, business consultants, and academicians have understood the limitations of measuring personal performance for decades. This has resulted in many changes over the years, mostly dealing with the methodology of the performance review. The result has been a litany of new, and ultimately flawed, performance evaluation processes, including trait scales, the descriptive essay, the behavioral checklist, the Behaviorally Anchored Rating Scale (BARS), Management By Objective (MBO), the critical incidents method, the 360-degree feedback method, and the forced ranking system.

In the end, however, I believe Scott Adams, author of *The Dilbert Principle,* got it right when he wrote,

"In theory, the Performance Review process can be thought of as a positive interaction between a 'coach' and an employee, working together to achieve maximum performance. In reality, it's more like finding a dead squirrel in your backyard and realizing the best solution is to fling it onto your neighbor's roof. Then your obnoxious neighbor takes it off the roof and flings it back, as if he had the right to do that. Ultimately, nobody's happy, least of all the squirrel."

If you're not getting the recognition you deserve on the job, you're not alone. And it may or may not be because you have a mean boss who plays favorites or is uninformed. Despite every effort to promote employees on the basis of merit, employers admit they make a mistake in four out of every ten promotions. So much for the meritocracy. The whole recognition process is flawed because it is reliant on fundamentally flawed assumptions: that personal performance and organizational performance are directly linked, and that personal performance is observable and can be objectively measured.

So, the problem is clear. Someone else may get the credit for your successes, and your contribution may never be fully recognized. On the face of it, frustration, disappointment, and disillusionment seem inevitable.

Thankfully, God provides a beacon of hope: The solution lies in a change in perspective. Consider the story of the workers in the vineyard, as told in the book of Matthew.

A Change in Perspective

The owner of the vineyard went out early one day and hired several men to work for the day. He offered, and they accepted, a wage for the day.

As the day went on, the owner continued to hire additional workers. The last group of workers, in fact, was hired with only an hour left in the workday.

All was well and good until it came time to pay the workers. Much to the annoyance of the workers who began early in the morning, the owner gave the same amount of money to everyone, including those who had arrived just an hour prior.

The workers who had worked the longest, not surprisingly, were angry at the perceived injustice and complained to the owner. He, however, pointed out that they had been paid exactly what they had agreed to be paid. They had not been cheated in any way. If he was guilty of anything, the owner was guilty only of generosity, which, of course, was his prerogative.

By American workplace standards of fairness, the workers who arrived early in the day clearly got cheated. They worked longer, contributed more, and by our expectations, should have received more in compensation than the workers who arrived late in the day.

Our secular model of fairness is based on the model of equal opportunity for all, a sub-model of the overall model of free-market capitalism. It's a spectacular model, really, because it encourages hope. More than any other model, and the alternative economic "isms" they have given rise to, the American model is the most powerful at generating optimism for the future, both individually and collectively.

Alas, it doesn't always work as theoretically intended. Equal opportunity is a frustratingly elusive goal at all levels of society. The workplace is no exception.

The problem is not in the model itself. As imperfect as it is, it is, arguably, the best model of fairness developed to date. Our discontent results from the way in which we value the outcome of the model.

When most of us think of fairness in the workplace, we think of things such as our income, our titles, our offices, and our status. The outcome by which we measure workplace fairness, in other words, is defined by results, and, more importantly, results that we value largely on a relative basis. In this regard, the American workplace culture mirrors American culture at large. From early childhood we are taught to achieve. We are taught to measure our lives by our accomplishments. We learn to measure success or failure by the yardstick of successful endeavors. Whether we're try-ing to score a goal on the soccer field, get good grades in school, or win the latest reality game show, we have a task-oriented perspective on life.

Modern America is a results-oriented society that values accomplishment above all else. We honor achievements, whether it's hitting the most home runs in a season or acquiring a great fortune through shrewd investing. We admire perseverance, fortitude, and dedication. We applaud drive and ambition.

The workplace is no exception. We are counseled to be results-oriented, to make things happen. Being la-beled a go-getter is a compliment. No one ever makes vice-president in corporate America today without a "record of achievement."

Our accomplishments often say little, however, about how fulfilling our lives are. Divorce and sub-stance abuse are certainly not confined to the poor and the unaccomplished. People who seem to lead incred-ibly fascinating and accomplished lives can be perpetu-ally miserable.

A man from India once worked for me as the head of one of our engineering departments. One year the company was having a rough go of it, and I had to inform him that there would be no money for raises for the people in his department. He said that he un-derstood and would do his best to keep his people motivated. He admitted, however, that this would be a difficult challenge.

"Since arriving here from India," he said, "it has always struck me that Americans equate wealth and happiness. We, of course, have a great deal of poverty in India, and Americans naturally assume that these people must be very, very sad. It is true that they often lead difficult lives, but many of them lead very fulfilling lives."

We Americans have gotten accustomed to calibrating things according to accomplishments. It's relatively quick and easy; it's efficient and we're busy. We take shortcuts, often judging a person on how they look, what they drive, where they live. It's a social yardstick that we learn from an early age. We all know an expensive mansion when we see one. And while most of us will never drive the most luxurious cars available, we all know what they look like. This, of course, is what the companies that make luxury products have trained us to do. We call it marketing, and a great deal of it today reinforces external standards of success and worth. Advertisers appeal to what a product or service will say about us rather than what it will do for us. But the external standards that motivate us are a mirage.

God, by contrast, measures achievement by a totally internal standard: our faith. Some of us set out on this journey early in life. Others find the path only late in their mortal lives. The ultimate message of the vineyard parable, however, is that those differences are irrelevant to God. In God's eyes, each of us has the same opportunity to achieve the ultimate success of admittance to the Kingdom. God's model is the quintessential equal-opportunity model.

Think of the phrase "holier than thou." It suggests that there are rankings of holiness, that holiness is something we achieve, rather than live. This is the attitude that the longest-serving workers in the vineyard had and reflects most workplace standards of achievement. These early-arriving workers who toiled longer, and achieved more, believed they deserved more of God's grace.

God, however, has a very different perspective on what is and is not fair—at least when it comes to grace. God gave these workers nothing less than he had promised and that they had expected. The source of their displeasure was strictly a relative one, based on the mistaken notion that God's grace (i.e., the compensation) is *earned* proportionately.

God obviously doesn't see it that way. Such a performance model would create nothing short of a spiritual caste system, not unlike the hierarchy we have in the workplace. We would each be spiritually rewarded at different levels.

Each of us who finds faith will know God's grace in equal measure. It doesn't matter when we arrive at that faith. It only matters that we do. It's never too late. God's grace, in other words, is not earned but given. Thankfully, from God's perspective, everyone is equal through faith.

Faith Is Not a Contest

We often treat life as a contest. Competition consumes us. Sports analogies fill our conversations. Put a motor on anything, and we will race it. Define beauty by body weight, and we will go to unhealthy lengths to thin down. Whatever we do, we strive to do it better than anyone else.

We even refer to people we admire as being "accomplished." We assume that a person who becomes a doctor or lawyer is worthy of our respect and deference. We assume that the person with the Ph.D. is smart and learned. And whether it's the CEO of a *Fortune* 500 company or a United States Senator, we naturally hold people who have "achieved" in high esteem.

God's model of reward and recognition, however, is not built on competition. Faith is not a contest. We can't store away our past faith under the mattress to cash in at the end of our days.

Faith is a state of mind that is acquired by opening our minds and our hearts to God, our thoughts and our perspectives to what really matters. It means that we don't have to rely on others for reward and rec-ognition. It matters little what others have concluded about us. It matters only that we have faith. Consider the following story from the book of Mark.

After healing a demon-possessed man, Jesus crossed the Sea of Galilee to Capernaum, where he was greeted by a large crowd. Out of the crowd came Jairus, one of the synagogue rulers, who begged Jesus to come with him so that Jesus might heal Jairus' dying daughter.

Jesus agreed. As they walked through the large crowd, however, a woman who had long suffered from incurable bleeding came up behind Jesus and touched his cloak. She was instantly cured, even though Jesus was unaware of who touched him.

No one else seemed to know either. Eventually, how-ever, the woman rushed forward, fell at the feet of Jesus, and confessed that it was she who had touched him without his permission. Jesus, however, was not offended or angry. Instead, he consoled the woman and told her that her faith had healed her.

Jesus then continued with his entourage to the home of Jairus. When they arrived, however, they were too late. The young girl had died, and the group gathered was wailing and mourning her loss.

Unfazed, Jesus told Jairus to have faith and then went to the young girl and awoke her. She, too, was instantly cured and got up and began walking around the room, to the astonishment of her parents.

This is a story about two very different healings. In one case, Jesus was asked by the synagogue ruler, a prominent citizen—a CEO, you might say—to heal the ruler's daughter. In the other, a woman in the crowd— an ordinary worker—was healed without Jesus' prior knowledge of her affliction or her desire to be cured.

To fully appreciate the significance of the woman's healing, we need to understand that she was not just an ill woman; she was a social outcast. By Old Testament law, she and anyone who touched her were considered "unclean."

Despite the fact that everyone looked down on her, Jesus granted the woman the same recognition that he granted the daughter of the ruler of the synagogue. He recognized the woman for what mattered most: her faith.

This is wonderful news. If we have faith, we will ultimately be recognized, despite what others may think of us or what recognition we receive in life. We do not need to compete for God's grace. There are no performance reviews that will gain us entrance into a first-class heaven, or put us back in a coach-class heaven. We will *always* be fully recognized for our faith.

In fact, God's model eliminates the need for competition. For if we walk with God, we will have succeeded in the only way that really matters.

Go back to the vineyard parable for a moment. The last line of the parable reads, "So the last will be first, and the first will be last." It would be easy to interpret that to mean that God will reward the downtrodden and punish the accomplished.

The more complete interpretation is that God does not rank any of us. The words "first" and "last" have no meaning to God. God values each of us individually and equally in a way that has nothing to do with any performance review.

Isn't that nice to know?

If you're angered and frustrated by the reward and recognition practices in your workplace, you probably have good reason to be, and you are certainly not alone. Your discontent, however, will do more to make your life miserable than it will to change those practices.

God, as always, has a better idea. God has given us a model of accomplishment devoid of rankings and subjective evaluations. God's equal-opportunity model gives each of us the exact same opportunity to succeed. We don't have to be pretty or handsome. We don't have to be athletic or strong. We don't have to be rich and powerful.

We need merely to walk with God.

And if we do, we will realize the ultimate reward: entry into the Kingdom of God.

CHAPTER FOUR

Coping With Overload

Christian Perseverance

Do you have too much work to do? Have you been asked to take on more work as your company cuts back on people?

You're not alone. In a study conducted by Harris Interactive on behalf of the Families and Work Institute, researchers found that more than half of employees felt overwhelmed by their workload at some point. The National Sleep Foundation found that the average employed American worked a 46-hour work week, and more than one-third routinely worked more than 50 hours per week.

In its latest bi-annual look at workplace trends in the U.S., the Economic Policy Institute found that the combined hours put in on the job by middle-income parents, ages 25–54, was up 11 percent since 1975. That works out to an additional *5 weeks* per year on the job.

Add to this all of the other increasing time demands put on America's modern families, and it's no wonder so many of us feel perpetually exhausted. According to the National Sleep Foundation's 2005 *Sleep in America* poll, only 26 percent of American adults are getting more than eight hours of sleep per night on weekdays. That's down from 38 percent in 2001!

So how do we deal with all of this work?

Destined to Work

Before we jump to the conclusion that work itself is the problem, we need to understand that the Bible makes it clear that work is our destiny. Consider what God said after discovering Adam and Eve had eaten the forbidden fruit:

> To Adam he said, "Because you listened to your wife and ate from the tree about which I commanded you, you must not eat of it.
>
> Cursed is the ground because of you;
>   through painful toil you will eat of it
>   all the days of your life.
> It will produce thorns and thistles for you,
>   and you will eat the plants of the field.
> By the sweat of your brow
>   you will eat your food
> until you return to the ground."
>
> Genesis 3:17–19a

That does not mean work is punishment and lacks dignity. There are numerous passages throughout the Bible that reference the spiritual nobility of work. Consider this proclamation of the Apostle Paul:

> You yourselves know that these hands of mine have supplied my own needs and the needs of my companions. In everything I did, I showed you that by this kind of hard work we must help the weak, remembering the words the Lord Jesus himself said: "It is more blessed to give than to receive."
>
> ACTS 20:34-35

Paul reinforced the idea in his letter to Titus:

> Our people must learn to devote themselves to doing what is good, in order that they may provide for daily necessities and not live unproductive lives.
>
> TITUS 3:14

In a similar vein, Paul wrote to the people of Thessalonica:

> Now we ask you, brothers, to respect those who work hard among you, who are over you in the Lord and who admonish you. Hold them in the

> highest regard in love because of their work.
> Live in peace with each other. And we urge
> you, brothers, warn those who are idle, encour-
> age the timid, help the weak, be patient with
> everyone.
>
> 1 THESSALONIANS 5:12–14

Clearly, work is expected of us. It is an important part of life. The key question is: What are we working *for*?

The Importance of Purpose

Ask someone what their life purpose is and, more often than not, they'll tell you how they like to spend their time, what they want to do for a living, or what accomplishments they hope to achieve. But they're giving you a desired *result*, not a purpose. They're telling you the *what*, not the *why*, of their lives.

A lot of the stress in the workplace is a simple matter of not having, or not understanding, life's purpose. When we look for work to provide a reason for being, either directly through achievement or indirectly through the rewards that accompany achievement, we are looking for work to fulfill a need it cannot possibly fulfill.

Said differently, a lot of people feel overwhelmed

by their work because they *need* to. They rely on their work for identity and self-esteem. Their work is who they are. They may actually have a personal incentive to feel overworked and stressed out. It reinforces the sense of importance they seek to get out of their work. After all, if someone is going to identify themselves as a juggler, won't they want to be a juggler who can juggle more balls than anyone else?

In my own case, I always thought of my ability to deal with an excessive workload as a yardstick of my personal discipline. If I could get through twenty tasks per day, even if I went home stressed out, I would nonetheless feel a certain sense of twisted accomplishment. Because I was relying on my ability to "handle" my job for my identity, I had little reason to set personal priorities. What would I devote the extra time to, anyway?

You might believe that you have not fallen into that trap because you can easily think of a million things you would like to do if only you had some free time. Perhaps you would like to play golf or relax with a good book. Perhaps you would just like to take a nap or get to bed at a more reasonable hour.

In the end, however, our need for identity, for self-esteem, cannot be satisfied through these desires. And if our need for identity is not being satisfied, playing golf and reading books just will not be as much fun anymore—not because we have grown bored with these activities, but because there is a more fundamental need not being met.

Leisure is not a life purpose any more than work is. No matter how much we enjoy an activity, or how good we are at it, our leisure activities cannot give us reason for being here. To be clear, I love sports. I love to participate in them. I love to watch them. I think athleticism is a thing of beauty. And I believe that professional athletes can lead holy lives. However, it is not what they do for a living, any more than it is what we do for a living, that makes life holy and gives life a purpose.

A purpose is an intended result or goal. It's the reason for doing something. We play golf, for example, because we expect it to bring us enjoyment and satisfaction. We comb or style our hair in order to improve our personal appearance. Nearly all results, however, are transitory. The enjoyment of a good round of golf eventually fades. When we rise tomorrow morning, we will have to comb or style our hair once again.

This is why work and leisure ultimately fall short of being fulfilling life purposes: They are ephemeral. They don't outlive us. When we cease to exist, so too do most of the results we've achieved and the pleasures we've enjoyed. So, too, do the transient "purposes" for which we have lived.

But if neither work nor leisure is a legitimate life purpose, what is?

Kurt Warner, the quarterback for the St. Louis Rams, and unlikely MVP of Super Bowl XXXIV, put the issue in proper perspective. Speaking to a crowd of 40,000, Warner said, "Who am I? I am not a football player. That is what I *do*. I *am* a devout Christian man."

The Apostle Peter put it this way:

It was not with perishable things such as silver or gold that you were redeemed ... but with the precious blood of Christ, a lamb without blemish or defect. He was chosen before the creation of the world, but was revealed in these last times for your sake. Through him you believe in God, who raised him from the dead and glorified him, and so your faith and hope are in God.

"All men are like grass,
    and all their glory is like the flowers
      of the field;
the grass withers and the flowers fall,
    but the word of the Lord stands
      forever."
And this is the word that was preached to you.
1 PETER 1:18–21, 24–25

There are two purposes whose results outlast our mortal lives. One is faith, which leads to eternal life. The other is service to others, which, broadly speaking, gives us a purpose larger than ourselves, a purpose that survives our existence. It is service, not achievement, that leads to true legacy. Faith and service, however, go hand in hand. Service to others is an important part of faith, and faith gives context to our service. Faith gives us the perseverance that is inevitably needed in a life of service.

While you may not consider your job as "serving others" in any spiritual sense, that same perseverance is essential to getting through the "daily grind." Life isn't always easy. We are challenged on a daily basis. We are challenged in our work. We are challenged in our relationships. We are challenged by our responsibilities as parents, siblings, or children. Without perseverance, these challenges can easily overwhelm us. Without perseverance, our joys can be obliterated by our burdens. We can become buried by our duties and obligations.

With perseverance, however, we can get through the trials of daily life. We can survive the challenges that stand before us. We can conquer those things that otherwise dampen our spirit or lessen our enjoyment of living. And it is through faith that we gain the perseverance to get through the tough parts and not be overwhelmed. By giving us something that outlasts the impermanent challenges of everyday living, faith gives us the strength to persevere.

Patience = Perseverance in Progress

If faith is the source of perseverance, then perseverance is the source of patience. Think of patience as perseverance in the here and now, as perseverance in progress.

Patience is not held in particularly high regard in the modern workplace. On the contrary, haste and urgency are encouraged, admired, and often rewarded. This emphasis on urgency, I believe, is a grossly mistaken perspective that leads to a great number of mistakes. And the reason is rather simple: Knowledge takes time.

What happens when there is a perceived crisis in your workplace? Chances are there's a meeting. And a lot of wringing of hands and unproductive speculation about what might or might not have happened. In the end, however, there is often little that can be done at that point in time because all the facts aren't in. Any attempt to act is likely to prove ineffective or inadvisable.

It's easy to get caught up in the emotion of the moment. In a culture that puts a premium on accomplishment, time is a very limited resource. Accomplishment requires action. And the time for action is finite.

An insightful colleague of mine is fond of saying, "When there's unexpected news, in the end it will neither be as good as we hoped nor as bad as we feared." In my experience, that is usually the case. When all the facts are known, most problems are not as serious as originally feared. The same is true of good news: The ultimate picture is not usually as rosy as the original sketch.

If we make a decision in haste, therefore, we're likely to make the wrong decision because we don't have enough knowledge yet. On the other hand, you might say, if we don't act quickly, we may lose the opportunity to act, or the conditions might get worse. And that, inevitably, is the reason that urgency is so highly valued in today's workplace.

Urgency and uncertainty go hand in hand. When there is a great deal of uncertainty about the future, the sense of urgency is heightened. We're inclined to fear the worst. We're inclined to believe that time is not on our side.

We're not comfortable with uncertainty. It makes us anxious. It fills us with foreboding. In such an environment, patience is hard to come by. Rather than taking time to clarify our decisions, we are tempted to act quickly and, perhaps, irrationally.

I've done it many times. I've killed great ideas before giving them the time to work. I've pulled new products that were on the verge of taking off. I've reassigned people who were on the brink of mastering a job I had concluded they could not do.

At the same time, however, I've been criticized for not acting quickly enough. I recall one occasion early in my career when the company was going through tough times, and every manager was required to reduce staffing immediately. The financial executive challenged me for not including one particular individual on the list of reductions. While this person was not a star performer, I thought he had a lot of potential, and I was willing to give him time to grow in his abilities.

Years later that individual ended up working for the executive who had challenged me. The executive thanked me for standing by this person because he was now one of the executive's most valuable employees.

This is where the value of faith comes in. Because faith gives us long-term values, faith also gives us patience. Because faith is a rock-solid connection to the eternal, faith gives us security. Faith gives us an "end game," to use a sports analogy popular in business today—eternal life—and a road map by which to get there. With faith, time is no longer the enemy.

This is why, in my experience, organizations that take the time to define their values often outperform organizations that don't. Making money is a desired outcome, but it is not a *value*. Companies that believe profitability is the only guiding light they need tend to make disjointed and often counter-productive decisions in haste. Companies that have established a set of institutional values, on the other hand, have the luxury of patience. Their values give them trail markers that provide re-assurance and eliminate the temptation of over-reacting to uncertainty.

Every worker, every organization, every company has to make decisions about what they value. And what they value will drive their priorities.

Priorities = Values in Action

Priorities are essential to efficiency and effectiveness. Both at home and on the job, if we don't have priorities, we quickly become overwhelmed and may find ourselves literally drowning in the possibilities. While actions are finite, the potential for action is infinite. The possible actions to be taken will always exceed the capacity to actually take them.

We cannot manage the infinite. Time, as it relates to our life or our workday, is finite. We have to narrow the possibilities for action to a finite list of actions that are achievable and will get us closest to our desired goal. We need to set priorities.

Many organizations, however, are very poor at setting priorities. That's particularly true for large organizations. Small organizations, in my experience, are far better at setting priorities and are, as a result, far more efficient. While it is often suggested that greater size leads to greater economies of scale, just the opposite is true when it comes to organizational efficiency.

There are two overriding reasons for this. The first is that larger organizations simply have more cushion. They can be less productive and still survive from sheer momentum. Small organizations typically don't have that luxury.

The second is that large organizations are dependent on a series of processes in order to function. Since the work can't all be performed by one person, or even a small team of people, processes have to be in place to break the workload down into manageable chunks. The problem is that these processes often take on a life of their own. As I discussed in my book *The Ultimate MBA: Meaningful Biblical Analogies for Business,* these processes often outlive their original purpose and divert the organization's attention from the end to the means. The process, in other words, ends up being the priority.

In principle, we may readily acknowledge that God

has already given us the priorities by which to live our lives. But can the priorities of our faith help us sort through a burdensome workload on the job? The answer is definitely yes. If the priorities of faith are the most efficient and effective way to run our lives, they must, by definition, be the most efficient and effective way to run our work.

At first blush, we may be reluctant to accept that logic. It's not what most of us have been taught. We've been conditioned to think of our personal lives and our work lives as separate and distinct. We've been conditioned to think that work and business are impersonal.

But what is God's greatest commandment? What is the one thing above all else that we must do in order to have a meaningful relationship with God?

> "Love the Lord your God with all your heart
> and with all your soul and with all your mind."
> This is the first and greatest commandment.
> And the second is like it: "Love your neighbor
> as yourself." All the Law and the Prophets hang
> on these two commandments.
>
> MATTHEW 22:37–40

The first of these two commandments is self-explanatory. And while it may not apply directly to our work, it supersedes it. Our relationship with God is more important than anything else, including our work.

In the book of Mark we are told the story of Jesus traveling to a town where all the sick and demon-possessed people of the town came to the home where Jesus was staying. He cured most of the sick and drove out most of the demons, but it eventually became late, and Jesus retired for the evening. In the morning, Jesus rose early and went off by himself to pray. His hosts, however, came looking for him, anxious for him to continue healing the people of the town.

From a theological perspective, many see this story as evidence that Jesus wanted to keep people focused on his ministry, not just on his healing. From a practical perspective, however, this story reinforces the importance of putting our relationship with God above all else. No matter how much work we have to do, or how many people have expectations of us, our relationship with God takes priority. Taking, or making, time to spend with God—even when there is "too much to do"—is paramount.

And that leads us to the second commandment: How does loving our neighbor relate to our work?

Part of the answer lies in why jobs exist in the first place. Whether we work for a big industrial corporation or a small non-profit charity, our job exists for the sake of using our time and skill to create or do something of value, however our organization defines it. And doesn't the creation of value inevitably involve service to others?

The other part of the answer lies in how we treat our co-workers each day—especially if we are working under time pressures and deadlines, or in tough circumstances. The priority is still clear: Love your neighbor as yourself.

If you attempt to posture and politic your way to the top, you will force your co-workers to do the same. In the end, it will be not so much a competition for you to win as it is for others to lose. If, on the other hand, you treat your co-workers as you want to be treated, they will have every incentive to do the same toward you.

In the end, the four "P's" of *purpose, patience, perseverance*, and *priorities* come down to this: If you take God to work, your faith will give your life a *purpose* and your work meaning. Faith will give you the *patience* to cope with the challenges you face and the workload that threatens to overwhelm you. Faith will give you the strength to *persevere* and will render your days less stressful. Faith will give you the values and the *priorities* you need to work efficiently.

That's the good news. The great news, however, is that no matter what business you are in, or what job you hold, your faith will make you more effective.

CHAPTER FIVE

Teamwork in the Workplace

Christian Connection

Is there a lot of talk about teamwork in your workplace? Is it sincere? Or are the banners on the wall, and the letters and speeches to employees about being part of one big, happy family, just constant reminders that you're really *not* "all in it together"?

I think I know how you'll answer. I was one of those people who gave the pep talks and wrote the folksy letters to employees. Though I was sincere in everything I said about the importance of teamwork, in time I realized that Scott Adams, creator of Dilbert, had it right when he said, "Team-building exercises come in many forms, but they all trace their roots back to the prison system. In your typical team-building exercise the employees are subjected to a variety of unpleasant situations until they become either a cohesive team or a ring of car jackers."

Yet if the typical American workplace commitment to teamwork is largely hollow, it's not some vast managerial conspiracy to deceive American workers. The problem is more fundamental. The reason that teamwork is not frequently achieved in the American workplace, despite the expenditure of billions of dollars on training, banners, and tee-shirts, lies in how employers typically define "teamwork."

The Workplace Model of Teamwork

Like everything else in the workplace, workplace teamwork is built around the idea of enhanced performance. If we work together, the theory goes, we will perform better than we will individually. It's a classic variation of the old axiom that the whole is greater than the sum of its parts. Coordinated, mutually supportive effort, it suggests, will generate greater results with the same number of people than uncoordinated individual effort. At its core, workplace teamwork is all about productivity, the lifeblood of business.

Employers borrow their concept of teamwork, in part, from the world of team sports. On an athletic team each member has an assigned role designed to complement every other role and, in total, to accomplish all of the tasks necessary for team success. All the team members have a vested interest in helping each other perform at the highest level possible. Athletic team members, however, share a simple and shared definition of success: winning the contest. In the most literal sense, the members of the team have a shared destiny that is immediate and tangible.

In the workplace, by contrast, team members share a common destiny in only the most casual sense. If the company fails, they may all lose their jobs. If the company succeeds, however, there is no guarantee that any member of the team will keep his or her job. And even if they do, they may not—and probably will not—receive the same reward and recognition as other members of the team.

While it is true that professional athletes are financially rewarded on individual performance, you might be surprised to learn that the spread between the highest-paid professional athletes and the average athlete in their respective leagues is substantially narrower than the same spread in the business world. And contrary to the typical workplace, the coaches, or "bosses," frequently make less than their star players.

The biggest hurdle to concurrently promoting teamwork and individual performance in the workplace is the inability to objectively measure individual performance and relate it to organizational performance. Individual performance is often clouded by the sheer number of participants, the complexity of the tasks, and the number of external factors that affect the results.

In team sporting contests, by contrast, there are

only a handful of players participating in the game at any one time. The tasks are relatively straightforward, and the environment is strictly controlled by rules and impartial officials to enforce them. A baseball player's batting average over the course of a season, for example, is an objective measure of how well the player has batted relative to the other players.

In the workplace, moreover, uncontrollable external forces, such as national economic policy and technological innovation, can have a tremendous impact on the outcome of a workplace contest between two competitors. It is entirely possible to have a great team in a business that is wiped out by globalization or by technological innovation that obsoletes the product or service.

There is, on balance, simply a far greater correlation between teamwork and organizational success in the world of sports than in the workplace. If a star NFL player wants a Super Bowl ring, he will have to be part of an outstanding team. He cannot attain that objective without the help of his team members.

In the workplace, however, if your objective is to get promoted, you may not need help from your fellow team members. While an obvious lack of support from your team members may affect your success, your supervisor may give little weight to that factor in deciding who is going to get rewarded and who isn't.

In fact, the workplace model of competition for recognition and reward often leads to the kinds of alliances and gamesmanship immortalized by the *Survivor* reality television series. Where competition is promoted among team members, competitive energies are as likely to be directed *against* fellow team members as they are to be used to promote the common good of the team. It's called workplace politics, and it exists, to varying degrees, in almost every organization.

You probably aren't going to change that reality any time soon. You can, however, adopt a fresh perspective on teamwork that will reduce your frustration with the state of competitive teamwork in your workplace. The Christian model of teamwork, built on the importance of personal connection, is as well-suited to the workplace as it is to the home or church.

To see the difference between competitive teamwork and Christian teamwork in action, look at the parable of the Good Samaritan.

The Christian Model of Teamwork

Jesus was speaking to a group when an expert in the law stood up and asked him to explain the prerequisites to achieving eternal life. As Jesus often did, he turned the question back on the man, and the man answered correctly, saying that faith and goodwill

toward others were the two most important requirements.

Wanting to show off his own expertise, however,
and perhaps wanting to embarrass Jesus, the man went
on to ask Jesus what it meant to show good will to
others, what constituted goodwill, and to whom should
it be shown.

In reply, Jesus told the story of a man who was
traveling down a remote road when he was attacked
by robbers. He was stripped of his clothes, beaten severely, and left by the side of the road.

Some time after the attack, a priest was walking
down the road and saw the half-dead man. Instead of
helping him, however, the priest crossed to the other
side of the road and walked right past. Soon after, another traveler, a Levite, or assistant priest, came down
the road and did the same thing.

Eventually, a Samaritan man came down the road.
Samaritans at the time were generally looked down
upon as ignorant heathens. However, unlike the priest
and the Levite, this Samaritan decided to stop and
help the wounded man. In fact, the Samaritan took
care of the man's wounds, put him atop his own don-
key, and took him to an inn. There he made arrange-
ments with the innkeeper to take care of the man,
paying the innkeeper out of his own pocket.

Both the priest and the Levite may have been good team players in the workplace sense of performance of their religious duties. The workplace model of teamwork, however, puts little emphasis on good will if it does not contribute directly to the work for which the team exists. In fact, the workplace model may inhibit good will and generosity. The priest and the Levite, for example, may have rationalized passing by the beaten traveler on the basis that they had other commitments and didn't want to let down other "team members" who were relying on them.

Said differently, the workplace team is more narrowly defined in terms of both membership and objective than is the Christian model. The former is exclusive and self-serving, while the latter is all-encompassing and selfless.

At one level, the parable of the Good Samaritan is one of many stories throughout the Bible that affirms the message "Talk is cheap." There is an important difference between the typical workplace interpretation of that axiom, however, and the Christian interpretation. In the workplace, we are what we accomplish. From the Christian perspective, however, what we accomplish is a reflection of who we are. Who we are, not what we accomplish, is what really matters. And what we do speaks volumes about the real person inside.

The priest and the Levite—whom we would have expected to be compassionate by profession—showed their real character by crossing the road and ignoring the injured traveler. By contrast, the Samaritan showed that he was, despite the expectations of the crowd listening to Jesus tell the story, a man of compassionate and selfless character.

The Samaritan, in essence, embodies the Christian model of teamwork. It's a model based not on self-centered winning or losing, but on selflessly giving your all and actively reaching out to others.

Giving Your All

For many sports purists, ironically, it's the Christian model of teamwork, not the competitive model found in most workplaces, that is at the heart of sport. It's a model summed up well by the motto "all for one, one for all" that Alexandre Dumas attributes to the trio of heroes in his literary classic, *The Three Musketeers.*

This model of teamwork was succinctly articulated by Gary Gaines, the coach of a small-town high school football team from West Texas, in the movie *Friday Night Lights* (based on the book of the same name by H. G. Bissinger). His team was in the unlikely position of playing for the state championship, but they were facing a team far bigger, faster, and seemingly unbeatable. As expected, Gaines's team was down at halftime, and the coach was attempting to rally them for the second half.

What really matters, he told his team in the locker room, is not winning or losing the game. What matters is being able to look your teammates in the eye at the end of the contest and know in your heart that you did everything you could, that you made no excuses and held nothing back.

That is exactly what the Good Samaritan did. He didn't care who the injured traveler was or who was watching. He didn't extend his kindness in anticipation of any benefit to himself. He didn't view his actions as an accomplishment that would earn him status and respect among his family and friends. He helped the man because it was the right thing to do, and by doing it, he was able to look others in the eye and know in his heart that he had given all he could. He had held nothing back.

Christian teamwork is a process that requires commitment. Without follow-through, good intentions are hollow. The Good Samaritan didn't simply bandage up the injured man and drop him off in the nearest village; he also arranged for the innkeeper to take care of him. He was "team building" in the truest sense, as his self-less actions connected him with the beaten man and the innkeeper to create a working and effective team of three.

In many ways, this model of teamwork is far more difficult to fulfill than the competitive/achievement model. The self-centered workplace model of teamwork is motivated by what we expect our work will ultimately do for us. But in the Christian model, connection to self is secondary to connection with others. The reward is less direct, less obvious, but it is infinitely more satisfying.

When I first began my writing career, I struggled to find anyone who would publish my work. I wrote dozens and dozens of articles and submitted them to every conceivable magazine, including many small circulation magazines I had never heard of before. After hundreds of rejections, one of my articles was finally accepted, for which I was paid $250. Rounded off to the nearest dollar, that worked out to roughly nothing per hour for the time I had put into it.

When I sat at my desk with that check in hand, however, it gave me more personal satisfaction than any paycheck I had ever received. I knew in my heart that I had given my best. A supreme effort is a supreme effort, regardless of the outcome. Even if your efforts aren't enough to win, or the spoils of our victory are meager, knowing in your heart that you did everything you could, knowing you held nothing back, can be supremely satisfying.

Reaching Out

The workplace prides itself on being a world of achievement, but ironically, when it comes to teamwork, passivity may be the winning strategy. Because every team member is competing for limited reward and recognition, there is little personal benefit to reaching out to help a team member. Passivity, or "not making waves," is all too often an effective strategy for "successful" workplace teamwork, the objective of which is simply to get ahead.

Christian teamwork, on the other hand, is proactive. We are called to reach out. Look at the story of the sheep and the goats, from the book of Matthew.

Jesus told a parable about a King dividing everyone on earth into two groups, as a shepherd would separate the Sheep from the Goats. The King would invite the group represented by the Sheep into the kingdom with this explanation: "For I was hungry and you gave me something to eat, I was thirsty and you gave me something to drink, I was a stranger and you invited me in, I needed clothes and you clothed me, I was sick and you looked after me, I was in prison and you came to visit me" (Matthew 25:35–36).

This righteous group, however, would be incredulous and wonder when, in fact, they had done any of these things for the Lord. The King's response would be simple: "Whatever you did for one of the least of these . . . you did for me" (Matthew 25:40).

The group represented by the goats, conversely, would be told that they did none of these things and so were being sent into the eternal fires. Equally incredulous, but for a very different reason, they would ask for specifics. And they would be told about the times they had given nothing to eat, nothing to drink; the times they did not invite someone in or clothe someone or take care of someone. The King's final pronouncement would be, "Whatever you did not do for one of the least of these, you did not do for me" (Matthew 25:45).

The message of this story is clear: *Inaction is not an option*. Leaving people alone is not an option. Being too busy to help is not an option. We are called to help wherever there is a need and whomever has it.

Unfortunately, in the workplace, it's easy to rationalize passivity toward our co-workers. It doesn't help that we are literally competing with them for reward and recognition; that we all have too much to do and too little time in which to do it; that we're frequently overwhelmed by our own challenges. We may tell ourselves that there is little we can do to help others anyway. Or we may fear that people will perceive us as self-serving, as a smug and self-righteous "goodie two-shoes." These, however, are self-centered excuses. While they may suffice when it comes to workplace teamwork, they are illegitimate when it comes to Christian teamwork.

In the story of the sheep and the goats, the righteous people made no excuses. They reached out and showed compassion to their neighbors when they didn't have to. They took action even when it offered them no immediate or obvious benefit.

The real difference between the righteous and the cursed, however, was one of perspective. The humble and selfless perspective of the righteous group led them to do the right thing. The cursed, by contrast, allowed their self-interest to dominate their perspective: They didn't do the right thing because they didn't think that there was anything in it for them.

The "right thing" is always the selfless thing. It doesn't mean that doing the right thing won't benefit us. But it does mean that whatever we do, we do it for the right reason. At the end of the day it's not about "us" or "them." It's all about God. God calls us to reach out, whether we'll be recognized for it or not. God will know what we did and why we did it. And so will we.

Reaching out doesn't have to be a grand gesture.

When I was in college, I spent a summer on Cape Cod with four friends. During the day, I worked for a mason who built spectacular fireplaces for expensive homes, and at night I bused tables in a local restaurant. It was an education in the connecting power of simple gestures.

Some customers completely ignored me and, in some cases, made my job considerably more difficult by not moving even slightly to give me access to the dishes they expected me to clear away. Other customers, by contrast, treated me with respect and tried to make my job easier by passing hard-to-reach dishes or leaning back to give me easier access in a tight squeeze. Their acknowledgment of my presence gave me a sense of connection and helped to make my job more enjoyable and less frustrating.

A father at one table went so far as to tell his children, "This is the hardest working guy in this place." He then looked at me and said, "I've been watching. You're a hard worker and that's going to get you places." More than thirty years hence, his simple gesture still brings a smile to my face and fills my heart with pride and satisfaction.

On another occasion when I was working in a factory, a worker and I were loading barrels of scrap metal weighing several hundred pounds each into a tractor trailer. The trailer was parked on a downward slope, making our task even harder. One load got away from me and was about to pin me against the wall of the trailer, where it would surely have broken several of my ribs. The other worker, an older man with only a few years left to retirement, ran to where I was and, at some risk for his own safety, helped me to get the barrel back under control.

Afterward, I thanked him for his help. I was, however, a little embarrassed. Sensing this, the man said nothing of the incident to me or anyone else. He didn't laugh about it in the break room with his friends or admonish me for not being careful enough or make fun of me for being smaller than he was. He simply said, "You're welcome," asked if I was all right, and went back to work.

Reaching out may pose some risks. Given the self-centeredness of business culture, truly selfless gestures may be met with skepticism. The fellow worker who needs our help may tell us to mind our own business. In the end, we can't control what the people we reach out to do; that's up to them. Yet, ironically, it is this very lack of control that is fundamental to Christ's commandment to reach out. By reaching out, even when our effort might be rebuffed or worse, we are surrendering to Christ's directive. We are taking a risk that, in the long run, is no risk at all.

And that, ultimately, is the real difference between

the workplace model of teamwork and the Christian model of teamwork. The workplace model, the what's-in-it-for-me model, is ultimately unsustainable. If we are motivated strictly by self-interest, what do we have when all is said and done? Our self-interests, in the end, evaporate in the same way that our mortal pleasures and accomplishments do.

The Christian model of teamwork, by contrast, leads to eternal life. The benefit is infinite. The results are forever sustainable.

The Power of Connection

In the end, the self-centered, achievement-based model of teamwork found in most workplaces will not do the job because it does not provide connection to the people around us. At best, the workplace model of teamwork provides a sense of some future and abstract shared destiny. It may even give us hope that we will accomplish more and rise further than we would on our own. At worst, however, it simply lays the groundwork for the emptiness of hypocrisy and sets the stage for a reward that is finite and ultimately perishes.

In the Christian model of teamwork, connection is a core value. Think of how many biblical references there are to the importance of our human relationships, to our husbands or wives, our children, our brothers, our sisters, our neighbors, and our fellow Christians. Consider this one eloquent passage from the book of Romans, where Paul writes:

> Just as each of us has one body with many members, and these members do not all have the same function, so in Christ we who are many form one body, and each member belongs to all the others.
>
> ROMANS 12:4–5

The church my family attends is very large and very service-oriented. Everyone is strongly encouraged to get involved in some capacity, large or small. In part, that's simply a reflection of the many demands of running a successful church. It's also, however, a recognition of how important connection is to faith and how difficult connection can be to achieve in a large church.

At first, I admit, I was hesitant to get involved. I am shy and quiet by nature and had previous experiences of offering to help only to be overwhelmed with demands. I also had numerous personal and professional responsibilities that allowed me to easily rationalize my inaction. Eventually, however, I gave in and signed up to work security in the children's area, which is a secure area of the building requiring special authorization for admission.

It was easy work and I love children, and I met a lot of new people who shared my Christian values and enthusiasm. What took me by surprise, however, was how much this small amount of service strengthened my faith. Simply by feeling more connected to others in the church, I acquired, in the most literal sense, an even greater connection to God.

And that, ultimately, is why Christian teamwork is so powerful. Reaching out to others brings both immediate and long-term benefits. It brings the joy of connection to people, and the personal fulfillment and hope that flows from a satisfying relationship with God.

CHAPTER SIX

Workplace Injustice

Christian Courage

Is your employer just? Do incompetent workers get rewarded while good workers get overlooked or taken for granted?

Despite all the talk about managing the workplace on the basis of merit, many employees are dissatisfied with their company's promotion and bonus practices. Few employees, it seems, believe that these practices are fair or objective.

It's a view, tellingly, that is also shared by their employers. In one recent survey, fully sixty percent of the companies polled admitted that they would not rehire their current management team if they were starting over. Three out of five promotions, in other words, are based on something other than true merit and ability.

It's the old Law of Reverse Consequence. In promoting *accountability* as the means to advancing performance, employers frequently suppress *productivity*. Time and energy are re-directed from solving problems to getting credit or assigning blame. Employees spend more time trying to impress the boss or covering their tracks than advancing the company's interests.

In a book entitled *Flawless Execution*, retired U.S. Air Force fighter pilot James D. Murphy compares the military's approach of enhancing job performance to the corporate approach. Take, for instance, the military's approach to debriefing when a mission goes wrong:

> Covering up a problem is idiotic, so when they talk about open communication, they mean open—nameless, rankless debriefs. When they cross the threshold of the briefing room door, they throw away their name and rank. All they bring in is truth, an open mind, and open communication. If there was a mistake, they want to freely admit it, in front of their peers, supervisors, or subordinates.

Is this what happens in your workplace? Probably not. And if it does, I can almost guarantee it's not the helpful learning process it should be.

The reason has to do with the myth of meritocracy. While the workplace is theoretically governed by personal performance, personal performance is almost impossible to measure. Merit, more often than not, is in the eye of the beholder, who has his or her own personally influenced perspective.

In the military, advancement is awarded by a very structured and methodical process. There are specific requirements for each promotion, and officers are promoted by independent peer review boards. Even a bad performance review can be appealed to a tribunal outside of the chain of command. This creates a very high level of consistency, fairness, and job security that, in turn, benefits both the military and its members. *Esprit de corps* is nurtured and performance enhanced. People are both effective and proud.

In the private sector workplace, by contrast, job security is essentially nonexistent. Time on the job, once recognized and rewarded, can now actually be a liability. Young employees often leapfrog older employees with more experience and seniority. Company loyalty, once nurtured and applauded, is now ignored, or worse. And too many years with one employer is likely to be seen by potential future employers as a lack of ability or ambition. There is no pretense of financial uniformity, and there are huge disparities in income within the average workplace.

In theory, of course, there are a lot of benefits to the ideal of workplace meritocracy. Employees can supposedly earn what they're "worth" and can rise as quickly as their abilities and ambition will carry them. Companies, in turn, are supposed to get better performance, since each job is theoretically filled by the best possible candidate.

In practice, however, that's not what usually happens. The flashiest employees, rather than the most capable, often get promoted. And companies frequently find that they've put the wrong people in the wrong jobs, creating a revolving door that severely hinders effectiveness

The sad reality is that any employee can easily be a victim of workplace injustice. There are few checks and balances. Employees are, in the most literal sense, at the mercy of their bosses. If, for whatever reason, that relationship is not ideal, or the boss's judgment is flawed, the employee pays the price in lost income and opportunity.

Unfortunately, you probably aren't going to change this reality any time soon. You can, however, make the most of the situation. You may not eliminate injustice in the workplace, but you can minimize its impact on you.

Have Courage

Consider the story of Queen Esther. In an improbable turn of events, this orphan Jewish girl, raised by her uncle Mordecai, was married to King Xerxes, who reigned over a vast kingdom that stretched from India to the upper Nile. Unfortunately, the king had a senior nobleman named Haman, who was very cunning and very influential—and who detested Mordecai.

In a plot worthy of a modern suspense novel, Haman tricked King Xerxes into issuing an edict to destroy all the Jews in his kingdom. When Mordecai heard about it, he went to Esther and tried to convince her to go to the king and persuade him to withdraw the edict and save the Jewish people. But there was a problem: No one, including the queen, was allowed to approach the king uninvited. He could overlook the infraction if he so chose, but the typical penalty for such a breach of protocol was death.

Not surprisingly, therefore, Esther was hesitant and told her uncle that she could not fulfill his request. Mordecai tried to change her mind, pointing out that her true identity would eventually be discovered and that she, too, would be killed unless the edict were rescinded.

Esther finally got up her courage and agreed to approach the king, even in the face of nearly certain death. The king, however, spared her, and in a strategic move, Esther invited the king and Haman to dine in her private quarters the following evening.

After laying the groundwork with two subsequent

evenings of private dinners, Esther was finally ready to make her courageous request: She asked the king to spare the Jews. The king became enraged—but not at Esther. Instead, he asked her who was behind the hideous plot. When she told him it was Haman, the king ordered his senior nobleman to be hanged on the very gallows that Haman had prepared to hang Mordecai. And the Jews were spared.

The story of Esther is a dramatic masterpiece, but its essence is something we all struggle with: How do we find the courage to do the right thing, even when the stakes and the potential consequences are far less extreme?

It's easy to rationalize inaction when faced with injustice, particularly if it doesn't affect us directly. We can always convince ourselves that we are powerless to right the wrong. We can always fool ourselves into believing that someone else will take care of it. We can always put dimensions on the injustice that make it appear trivial and inconsequential.

In reality, however, no injustice is minor. Small injustices inevitably grow into big ones and someone gets hurt. As Mordecai explained to Esther, no one is safe from injustice—*any* injustice. Injustice, like a lie, grows over time until it takes on a life of its own, engulfing everyone even remotely associated with it. If Esther had not gone to the king to save the Jews, she may have been spared in the short term, but she would eventually have suffered the same fate.

Workplace injustice often starts small. People get credit they don't deserve. Or somebody deserving *doesn't* get credit. An employee, sometimes the boss, allows personal bias to affect his or her working relationship with another employee. Or someone spreads a rumor or repeats a falsehood.

Left uncontested, these things can poison the workplace environment, destroying morale and making life difficult for everyone involved. They can pervade interactions and undermine the trust necessary for organizational effectiveness. By not standing up to injustice, however small, we end up allowing people like Haman to rule the day and trample justice.

With every injustice, we face the same questions Esther must have asked herself: How will this affect me if I confront it? How will it affect me if I *don't*? And, like Esther, we need to find the courage to choose on the side of doing the right thing.

Be Respectful

Admittedly, it's not always easy to address injustice in the workplace. The offending party may tell you to mind your own business, or they may even turn their wrath on you.

There are ways of getting involved, however, that will minimize the potential backlash and maximize your effectiveness. Most of them have to do with treating others as you would like to be treated. Whether or not the other person is truly deserving of deference or respect doesn't really matter. If we stoop to their level, our behavior is no better than theirs.

When Esther addressed the injustice with the king, she didn't barge into the inner court and say, "King, you idiot, you must spare the Jews, or I won't be your queen anymore." Instead, she approached him with respect and deference, even honoring him with a private dinner invitation.

Civility goes a long way. We all want to be treated with courtesy and respect. When we're not, we put up our guard and are less likely to digest the news objectively. We're more likely to lash back at the messenger.

This is why I always counsel people not to have difficult conversations while they're still upset or angry. A cooling-off period is in everyone's interests. A calm, collected mind will help you to sort out what's exaggerated or misrepresented, to digest and understand the information.

To respect someone is to give them the benefit of the doubt. Suppose someone comes to you with information that appears to reflect poorly on someone else. You have an obligation to that someone else to make sure you have all the facts before you run off and take action or further the misimpression.

That's not always easy to do in the workplace. There's always a sense of urgency to take action when a problem arises, and facts can sometimes be difficult to come by. Why did you, as a salesperson, for example, fail to meet budget this month? That's a complicated question that may have no simple answer. You may have not worked hard enough. But you may have not been provided with the right products at the right prices. The marketplace may have been soft. A major customer may have made a colossal mistake that affected its orders.

In the end, when it comes down to figuring out what really happened, we are frequently limited to opinions. What few facts exist are open to interpretation. It is imperative, therefore, that we show respect for everyone involved and not rush to judgment.

Unfortunately, I once worked for a boss who frequently rushed to judgment. He rationalized his rash behavior: He was, in his mind, a man of action. And it's commonly believed that this is a good thing when it comes to the workplace.

But you can imagine the results. He forced people to spend a lot of time and effort defending themselves. And he often made decisions in haste that ultimately had to be reversed, often at great cost to the company.

Respect isn't just a function of what we say. It's also a function of what we do. To be respectful is to act civilly and responsibly. When we show respect for others, both in what we say and how we say it, we will be shown the same respect in return. In the end, a respectful workplace will always be more productive and more effective than a disrespectful one.

Have Faith

That the unworthy sometimes win out over the worthy is not an injustice confined to the modern workplace. It's been around since the beginning of time.

Consider the Old Testament story of the prophet Habakkuk, who was dealing with the Babylonian Empire's invasion of the southern kingdom of Judah in 605 BCE. The Babylonians were a corrupt and sinful lot. Their success on the battlefield offended the virtuous sensibilities of Habakkuk, so he repeatedly asked God to strike them down and correct the injustice.

God, however, didn't appear to be listening. And when God finally did answer, it wasn't what the prophet expected or wanted to hear. God told Habakkuk, "I am raising up the Babylonians, that ruthless and impetuous people, who sweep across the whole earth to seize dwelling places not their own. They are a feared and dreaded people; they are a law to themselves" (Habakkuk 1:6–7).

With understandable indignation, Habakkuk demanded to know, "Why . . . do you tolerate the treacherous? Why are you silent while the wicked swallow up those more righteous than themselves?" (Habakkuk 1:13).

Once again, however, God dismissed Habakkuk's complaint and told him to have faith. And while it was true that the Babylonians were unjust and immoral and unworthy of success, God assured him that they would eventually get their due. "For the revelation awaits an appointed time . . . the Lord is in his holy temple; let all the earth be silent before him" (Habakkuk 2:3, 20).

In an incredible declaration of faith, Habakkuk finally accepted God's plan, trusting God's sovereign purpose: "I stand in awe of your deeds, O Lord. Renew them in our day; in our time make them known. . . . I will wait patiently. . . . The Sovereign Lord is my strength . . . he enables me to go on the heights" (Habakkuk 3:2, 16, 19).

Can you relate to Habakkuk's impatience with God? Have you ever seen some obvious injustice in your workplace to which you see a clear solution, and you can't understand why no one is addressing the issue? Does the injustice make you angry? Does it challenge your faith?

What Habakkuk didn't know was that God, in fact, was dealing with the Babylonians' moral injustice.

God had a plan, even though it wasn't the approach that Habakkuk would have taken or on the timetable that Habakkuk would have liked. God simply asked Habakkuk to have faith.

A man who had attended a very prestigious business school once told me his story. Upon graduation, he wanted to put his newly acquired knowledge to work and to thank his father, who had paid for his education.

His father owned a small business, so the son told his father that he would look at the father's business practices and give him the benefit of what he had learned. Which he did.

In his analysis, the son discovered that the father spent very little time trying to collect past-due bills from his customers. "That isn't right," the young man said. "You should go after them and collect the money you are owed."

To which the father replied, "Son, God will take care of the people who don't pay me. It's my job to take care of my good customers, not to punish the bad ones."

There's a reflection in this story of the real beauty of faith. With faith, we acquire a perspective that sees injustice through God's eyes. With faith, we can turn the anxiety and stress that injustice inflicts on us over to God. With faith, we can rely on God to do the right thing. With faith, we can know that justice will ultimately be served. If not today, then tomorrow. If not in one way, then another.

Have Patience

There is another important message for the workplace in the story of Habakkuk. It's the message of patience.

Wouldn't it be nice if no business ever failed, if each of us was assured of a job, and we all got promoted at the same time? We'd have to come up with another name for work!

But that, of course, is never going to happen. Change is a constant in our modern world, and change is a knife that cuts both ways. Sometimes we benefit from change. Sometimes we suffer from it.

If we try to anticipate change and act pro-actively, we may be wrong. The change may not occur, or it may occur in a different way than we had anticipated.

Or we may wait for the change to occur, but then react too quickly when it does. A lot of change proves to be temporary. And even when it's not, the true nature of the change isn't immediately apparent. Sometimes as it unfolds we see change for something very different than we did in the beginning.

Patience, in the end, is more than a virtue. It can be the most effective way to react to change. What would have happened to Habakkuk if he had lost patience with God and abandoned his faith? Would he have been better off? Would he have been able to punish the Babylonians and correct the injustice any more quickly or effectively?

I venture to guess that the only thing Habakkuk would have accomplished would have been the elimination of his faith. He would have gained nothing on the Babylonian front. He would have only given up what he had.

I once worked with a marketing colléagué who was very experienced in our business. He began to frustrate me, however, because every time I thought I had a new idea, he would point out that it had been tried before and failed.

One day I finally confronted him with my frustration. I'll never forget his response. He said, "Just because it didn't work before doesn't mean I don't think we should try it again. Things change. Maybe we just weren't patient enough."

During all of my nearly thirty years in business, I can safely say that the most common mistakes I've witnessed come down to a lack of patience. How many times has your company pulled a new product that wasn't performing up to expectations, but a competitor later had great success with it? How many times has your company concluded that something wasn't working, made a change, and discovered that it had been on the right track to begin with? How many times do you think employees have been passed over due to a perceived lack of growth potential only to go on to great success elsewhere?

Let's face it: Taking action is a whole lot more enticing than being patient. Action gives us a chance to prove ourselves. It gives us a chance to win. But in the end, like Habakkuk, we could lose what we have. More often than not, the penalty for waiting too long is a lot less severe than the penalty of a premature action that proves to be a mistake.

Thankfully, God's timing is not the same as ours. Our short-term "fix it" approach pales in comparison to God's eternal grasp of justice. That doesn't mean we should not take any action. But, rather, that we see our actions in a broader perspective—and trust God for the outcome.

Be Honest

Habakkuk obviously had his doubts. But he spoke up! He complained to God, even challenged God.

This gives us another biblical lesson for dealing with injustice in the workplace: Be open and honest in all communication. Don't embellish; don't fudge the truth; but say what needs to be said.

When people tell me that they are afraid to speak

up at work, I usually ask them if they really want to work at a company that punishes truth. If they answer in the negative, which they usually do, then I ask them what they're afraid of. If they tell the truth, and they tell it in a civil and professional way, what's the worst that can happen? They'll get fired from a job with a company that they don't want to work for.

In the end, few people get fired for bringing injustice to light. Most bosses value honesty, not just because everyone likes to work with honest co-workers, but because honesty is in their best interests. And most bosses know it. They can't take care of problems they're not aware of. And if they act on inaccurate or incomplete information, they're likely to make a mistake.

That's not to say that you should complain about every little problem. Nobody likes a cry-baby. And it does little good to point out the obvious. It's patronizing. If, however, you have something constructive to say, say it. Don't beat around the bush, even if you're embarrassed or you don't think it's what the boss wants to hear. You can't say something and *not* say it at the same time. If it *doesn't* need to be said, don't say it. If it *does* need to be said, don't open the door to misinterpretation.

A good friend was recently in the hospital with a very serious illness. I visited him on a couple of occasions and, as was my custom, I tried to be reassuring and empathetic while remaining straightforward. I didn't want to make him feel worse than he already did about his situation, but I didn't want to lie to him either. It would have been offensive to have said anything he knew wasn't true—even if he would have liked it to have been true!

Some time later, he thanked me for my visits. And he specifically thanked me for my candid comments and observations. He said that many visitors had tried to be reassuring to an extent that was unrealistic or untenable. While he appreciated their intent, their inflated and largely unfounded reassurances made him wonder if they really understood what he was going through.

Frankly, I had to learn this lesson the hard way. It's natural to be circumspect when the message you're trying to deliver might not be a welcomed one. A very capable female executive put me straight. She said, "You know, I appreciate the fact that you don't want to hurt my feelings or offend me in any way, but I sometimes have a hard time understanding what it is, exactly, that you want me to do. I'd prefer you'd just make it clear, even at the risk of hurting my feelings."

She was right, of course. I wanted people to like me and respect me. I still do. That's not a bad objective, as far as it goes. But it doesn't go far enough if it isn't honestly achieved. Otherwise, we've just contributed to another workplace injustice.

The good news is that honesty is a choice that we can make again and again. It's a choice that can make a daily difference—and have a long-range impact—on the side of good.

In the end, your workplace injustice may outlive your time there. That does not mean you should look the other way or sweep injustice under the rug. God's call is to have courage, have respect, have faith, and have patience. Ultimately God's sovereign purpose will prevail.

CHAPTER SEVEN

Overcoming Disappointment

Christian Character

What kinds of disappointment have you experienced on the job? Perhaps you didn't get the job evaluation or promotion you thought you deserved. Or maybe you were given a smaller raise than you expected. Or your plant announced it was closing. Or your shift got changed. Or your small business didn't meet sales expectations.

Disappointment starts early in life and follows us through childhood, adolescence, into adulthood and on into the workplace. There is no avoiding it.

Why is there so much disappointment?

The simple answer is that nobody knows the future. When we anticipate the future, as we are naturally inclined to do, we will sometimes be wrong. And when we anticipate something good happening to us, which we are also inclined to do, we will, on those occasions when we are wrong, be disappointed.

Disappointment is a fact of life for all of us. And

because of the nature of the environment and the stakes involved, the workplace, in particular, brings each of us more disappointment than we'd like.

I tend to take disappointment personally. I let it get me down. When that happens, I remind myself that I'm viewing my disappointment in terms of a problem rather than an opportunity. But disappointment can be a powerful teacher—if we are open to its lessons.

Disappointment presents an opportunity for us to grow spiritually, emotionally—*and* in our careers. In fact, I would go so far as to say that, just as a child who is never disappointed will never acquire the attitude necessary to lead a productive and fulfilling life, so, too, we cannot realize our full emotional, spiritual, and career potential without ever having experienced—and grown from—disappointment. Disappointment is not only the catalyst that precipitates character growth, it is *critical* to the development of character.

I think Helen Keller summed it up beautifully:

Character cannot be developed in ease and quiet. Only through experience of trial and suffering can the soul be strengthened, vision cleared, ambition inspired, and success achieved.

Are you aware of the manner in which muscle is built through exercise or hard physical labor? New muscle isn't just layered onto the old muscle. Some part of the old muscle is actually destroyed initially. (That's why we're sore after a strenuous workout.) Our bodies learn from the experience, however, and the muscle grows back to be even bigger than it was before.

If we never exercise or use our muscles, on the other hand, they atrophy. They wither away to the point that they are useless and ineffective. If we want to perform a task that requires strength, we won't be able to.

Our character is much the same way. If our character is never tested, or "exercised," it is naturally inclined to atrophy. Building character takes work. It's not always easy. It's not always painless. Like working out, it takes discipline and commitment.

Let's face it: Who really enjoys the actual process of getting in shape? What we enjoy is what it *does* for us. We enjoy how it makes us feel. We have more energy when we're in good physical shape. Our mood is better. We enjoy better overall health.

The same is true with character building. When we can use disappointment as an opportunity to learn, we can get into "emotional shape." Every disappointment offers us a chance to develop a healthier character.

The Lesson of Humility

One of the first lessons disappointment teaches us is humility.

You may have thought you were the obvious candidate for the promotion, or you may have already planned on a bonus you felt you deserved, or you may have prematurely celebrated the landing of a new account, only to have the promotion or bonus or deal fall through. If you've experienced this, you know how disappointing it can be—and how humbling.

If we were never disappointed, it would be easy to become arrogant and self-centered. We might begin to think we could never fail, that we could do whatever we wanted, that everything was within our grasp or control.

No one likes to be around someone who has let their blessings go to their head. No one likes to be around arrogant people. We instinctively know that arrogant people cannot truly see us because they're looking only at themselves. Arrogance, in effect, is the dividing line between selfishness and selflessness. It is, if you will, the barrier between looking in and looking out.

That is why humility is so important to faith. Arrogance not only separates us from other people, it also puts a barrier between us and God. Humility is the hammer that breaks down that wall.

For whoever exalts himself will be humbled,
and whoever humbles himself will be exalted.
MATTHEW 23:12

Webster's defines humble as "not proud or arrogant,"
which suggests that humility is a state of lacking, a
state of *not* being. The word "humble," however, comes
from the Latin word "humus," which means "earth."
To be truly humble, in other words, it is not enough *not*
to be arrogant or snooty. We must *be* humble.

Disappointment is a reactive and inward-looking
emotion. Humility, by contrast, is pro-active and
outward-looking. Disappointment is all about us.
Humility is all about God.

Humility is an important building block of Christian character because it turns our gaze outward.
Humility, nurtured in the fertile ground of disappointment, allows us to change our perspective. Humility is
the looking glass through which we see what we *have*
rather than what we *don't*.

As polar opposites, disappointment can help us
build humility, just as vigorous exercise helps us to
turn the destruction of muscle into greater strength.
That requires, however, that we grow in our disappointment, that we learn from our unhappiness. It
requires that when things don't go our way, we don't

wallow in our sorrow, we let it serve as a reminder that we are a part of God's creation—the earth itself.

The Lesson of Self-Reflection

Many times when we're disappointed, it has very little to do with what we have done or not done. Especially in the workplace, decisions are made that are beyond our control. The area where we do have control, however, is how we will respond to the disappointment.

For example, if you get passed over for a promotion, only you can decide what to do next. Will you try harder? Will you take some additional classes to enhance your skills? Will you consider changing career paths and entering a field that is better suited to your skills or where there are more opportunities? Or will you wallow in your disappointment? Will you allow anger and bitterness to poison your attitude and destroy your relationships with friends, family, and co-workers?

Your choice will depend, in large part, on your willingness to reflect on what has happened.

Disappointments present opportunities to take stock of ourselves. When we take the time to reflect on our disappointment—how we might have done things differently, how we might want to handle the disappointment, how our disappointment might help us move in a different direction—we can turn the pain of disappointment into a roadmap for self-improvement.

This is very much in line with the many references throughout the Bible regarding the importance of self-reflection and assessment.

> Examine yourselves to see whether you are in the faith; test yourselves. Do you not realize that Christ Jesus is in you—unless, of course, you fail the test? And I trust that you will discover that we have not failed the test. Now we pray to God that you will not do anything wrong. Not that people will see that we have stood the test but that you will do what is right even though we may seem to have failed. For we cannot do anything against the truth, but only for the truth.
>
> 2 CORINTHIANS 13:5–8

Self-reflection is a process of looking inward, but it goes deeper than the "what did I do wrong" level. Self-reflection can be the first step toward understanding "how can I be a better person." In self-reflection, we *look* inward to *act* outward.

Self-reflection, in other words, is the process by which we take what is beyond our control and grasp control of it. While the circumstances precipitating our disappointment may be beyond our control, our response to it is always within our control. We can examine our response, understand our reactions, and choose our attitude—and our future course of action.

When my book *The Ultimate MBA* was published, my very own church declined to carry it in the bookstore. I, of course, was deeply disappointed. I felt a deep sense of rejection. It was very difficult not to be embittered. My wife and I went so far as to attend an open house at another church nearby, thinking that we might switch our church home.

Thankfully, however, there was a little voice in my head that prompted me to think through my disappointment. At first my thoughts were devoted to trying to understand and explain the reason for the church's decision. Then I realized that I would never know for sure. No matter the reasons, it was a decision beyond my control.

So I turned the spotlight on myself. I candidly and objectively analyzed my relationship with God and the role that my church played in that relationship. I beseeched God in the same way that the psalmist did:

> Search me, O God, and know my heart;
>> Test me and know my anxious thoughts.
> See if there is any offensive way in me,
>> And lead me in the way everlasting.
>
> Psalm 139:23–24

And what did I find? I found that I was allowing an institutional decision to distract me from my relationship with God. As a result, I decided not to leave the church, but instead to become more involved. I volunteered to work in the children's program.

Did that cause me to be less disappointed? Not really. I still wish they had made the decision to carry the book. My disappointment sometimes wells up momentarily when I walk by the store's big display windows on Sunday morning.

It has, however, allowed me to get beyond my disappointment. As I became a more pro-active member of my Christian family, I was better able to appreciate all that my church offered. Instead of focusing on the disappointment it had caused me, I came to see the opportunity it presented to be part of a supportive Christian family and to build my relationship with God.

Disappointment always offers us an opportunity to take stock of our character and, in turn, our faith. We always have the choice to use disappointment as a springboard to growth.

The Lesson of Discipline

The word "discipline" has several connotations. It can refer to a form of character that allows us to act in a pre-determined way, to act in a way that we might not otherwise, because we have trained ourselves well.

Discipline can also be a *method* by which we train ourselves, or others, to act in a disciplined way. In other words, we use discipline to instill discipline.

Disappointment can be a form of educational discipline. When parents tell a child, for example, that ice cream is not for breakfast, they may be disappointing the child, but they are also teaching the child how to lead a healthier life.

God often does something similar. Consider the passage from the book of Deuteronomy in which Moses, having just delivered the Ten Commandments, was speaking to the people of Israel:

> Be careful to follow every command I am giving you today, so that you may live and increase and may enter and possess the land that the Lord promised on oath to your forefathers. Remember how the Lord your God led you all the way in the desert these forty years, to humble you and to test you in order to know what was in your heart, whether or not you would keep his commands. He humbled you, causing you to hunger and then feeding you with manna, which neither you nor your fathers

had known, to teach you that man does not live on bread alone but on every word that comes from the mouth of the Lord. Your clothes did not wear out and your feet did not swell during these forty years. Know then in your heart that as a man disciplines his son, so the Lord your God disciplines you.

DEUTERONOMY 8:1–5

That is not to suggest every time things don't go our way, God is disciplining us. That is to suggest, however, that we can use our disappointments as an opportunity for growth. The key lies in this phrase: *"to test you in order to know what was in your heart."* The discipline of disappointment is the ultimate self-reflection, a chance to test our character.

Is a test a punishment? It can seem like it if the subject matter is of no interest to us. But if we are interested, a test can be an enabler. It can help us learn and grow, even if we fail. In fact, we often learn more from our failures than our successes.

When I was a young boy, I took a test at school that included the following question: Which weighs more, a pound of feathers or a pound of nails? I quickly and confidently circled "nails" on the answer sheet. I, of course, was wrong. The correct answer was "neither."

I remember this failure vividly forty years later. It's one of those moments I would just love to grab out of the time continuum and do over again. I'm convinced, however, that this one failure has helped me to avoid many others. It taught me to be more careful before I respond, and that's a lesson that has served me well.

Consider this passage from the book of Hebrews:

My son, do not make light of the Lord's discipline,
      and do not lose heart when he rebukes you,
because the Lord disciplines those he loves,
      and he punishes everyone he accepts as a son.

Endure hardship as discipline; God is treating you as sons. For what son is not disciplined by his father? If you are not disciplined (and everyone undergoes discipline), then you are illegitimate children and not true sons. More-over, we have all had human fathers who disciplined us and we respected them for it. How much more should we submit to the Father of our spirits and live! Our fathers disciplined us for a little while as they thought best; but God disciplines us for our good, that we may share in his holiness. No discipline seems pleasant at the time, but painful. Later on, however, it

produces a harvest of righteousness and peace
for those who have been trained by it.

HEBREWS 12:5–11

"A harvest of righteousness and peace." That's hardly
what we think of when the boss assigns us an unpleasant task! The boss's perceived discipline is likely
to lead to indignation because, as adults, we are less
accustomed to being disciplined than when we were
young.

But don't we discipline our children so that they will
behave in a more disciplined manner when they are on
their own? So it is with us. We can react to disappointment with anger or insult—or we can use it to discipline
ourselves in a way that will bring us closer to God. We
can turn our disappointment into seething rage—or we
can use the experience to practice forgiveness and perseverance. We can react, and be unhappy—or act, and
grow.

The Lesson of Opportunity

Perhaps the most natural reaction to disappointment is
to focus on what *didn't* happen. But perhaps the most
valuable lesson of disappointment is to teach us to look
at what *can* happen. This is the lesson of opportunity.

Many famous people experienced disappointment before their success: Thomas Edison invented furniture made of cement, and then a perpetual cigar, before he invented the light bulb. Michael Jordan was cut from his high school basketball team. Henry Ford went bankrupt five times before realizing success. Lucille Ball was dismissed from drama school for being too shy. Abraham Lincoln lost eight elections, failed in two businesses, and had a nervous breakdown before becoming one of the most famous presidents in U.S. history.

Each of these people found a way to turn disappointment into opportunity. And all opportunities have one thing in common: They require that we take some action. An opportunity is only that—an opportunity. If something favorable happens of its own accord, it's a gift, not an opportunity.

When I first became a corporate president, the board of directors granted me certain powers that were necessary to do the job. I could sign checks, for example, and enter into contracts on behalf of the company. What they didn't do, however, was make me a good corporate president. They only gave me the *opportunity* to be one. Whether or not I was one was up to me.

Think about the lesson of opportunity the next time you are feeling disappointed about the lack of a promotion or salary increase. Even if your boss is sincere and diligent in monitoring the work of everyone in the work group, there are only so many hours in the day, and he or she can't be everywhere at once. Besides, he or she has a lot of other responsibilities to carry out.

At some point, therefore, if you want to get credit for your ability, you will have to make some effort to demonstrate it. Having it isn't enough. That doesn't mean that you should spend your days telling your boss how great you are. There's a difference between taking advantage of an opportunity and being an opportunist. Nonetheless, opportunities are generally worthless without action.

That's the bottom line. We have to act.

I think God wants faith to be a verb, not an adjective. Christian character is a matter of how we live, not what we think. Throughout the Bible we are implored to *do*, to act on our faith. In fact, according to *Strong's Exhaustive Concordance*, the word "do," or one of its derivatives, is used nearly fourteen-hundred times throughout the Old and New Testaments.

Here is but one of those occasions, but it is particularly powerful:

Blessed are they who maintain justice,
who constantly do what is right.

PSALM 106:3

Ultimately, Christian character is diligent, not dormant. It's active, not passive. Whether it's behaving morally or living charitably, it's doing something rather than nothing. We can't always control what is done to us, but we can control what we do. We can always turn disappointment into opportunity.

The Lesson of Hope

In the end, the fact that disappointment can always be turned into opportunity is the essence of Christian hope. Consider this passage from Paul to the people of Corinth at a time when he and his fellow Christians were being persecuted and false prophets abounded:

> Therefore we do not lose heart. Though outwardly we are wasting away, yet inwardly we are being renewed day by day. For our light and momentary troubles are achieving for us an eternal glory that far outweighs them all. So we fix our eyes not on what is seen, but on what is unseen. For what is seen is temporary, but what is unseen is eternal.
>
> 2 Corinthians 4:16–18

"*Do not lose heart.*" If you're worried about problems at work, or dismayed by prospects for your career, this message is for you. No matter what disappointments consume you, you always have the hope bequeathed to you through God's love. It's a definite, a sure thing. There is no doubt. With faith, you always have hope.

According to etymologists, or word historians, the English word "hope" is of unknown origin. Some, however, suggest a connection to the word "hop," as in "leaping in expectation."

True or not, I rather like that theory. It does justice to hope's potential. It recognizes the boundless energy of hope. With hope, anything is possible.

The connection between "hope" and "hop," moreover, reinforces the active nature of faith. It fortifies the notion that faith, and the hope that faith delivers without fail, is a state of *doing*.

In the end, disappointment cannot deprive you of hope. Disappointment is defenseless against faith. Disappointment is a mortal thorn that cannot pierce the armor of hope that God shields you with. This passage from the book of Romans sums it up perfectly:

> Therefore, since we have been justified through faith, we have peace with God through our Lord Jesus Christ, through whom we have gained access by faith into this grace in which we now stand. And we rejoice in the hope of the glory of God. Not only so, but we also

rejoice in our sufferings, because we know that suffering produces perseverance; perseverance, character; and character, hope. And hope does not disappoint us, because God has poured out his love into our hearts by the Holy Spirit, whom he has given us.

ROMANS 5:1–5

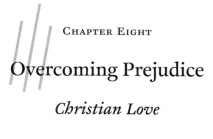

Chapter Eight

Overcoming Prejudice

Christian Love

Despite reams of new legislation designed to stamp it out, prejudice remains alive and well at many levels of the modern American workplace. Only ten of the companies listed in *Fortune* magazine's 2005 listing of America's five-hundred largest corporations are run by women. Only three are run by African-Americans.

But prejudice comes in many more forms than gender and ethnicity. We are often judged by such irrelevant factors as our height, our weight, our physical appearance, our social origins, our appearance, or our speech.

Not all prejudice is personal and purposeful; much of it is institutional. In the case of gender bias, for example, I honestly believe that the male chauvinist is a dying breed. Most men want to see women have equal opportunity in the workplace. The problem is that the American workplace was built by men. Naturally, they built it in their image. They built it around their values, beliefs, methods of communication, and life perspectives. Even when workplace diversity is sincerely embraced, therefore, the processes of reward, recognition, and advancement inadvertently disadvantage those who aren't built from the same mold.

This is, for example, why the American workplace remains such a difficult landscape for career-oriented mothers to navigate. The men who created the American workplace, who typically did not take primary responsibility for child-rearing, did not design a workplace institution that gave equal weight to child-rearing and career ambition. Working mothers, as a result, are frequently forced to make difficult choices between these two roles. If women had designed the workplace, it's safe to say, working mothers would not be under the stress they are today.

In the same vein, the men who created the modern workplace created an institution where competition and conquest are valued over compassion and interpersonal connection. This, too, has directly and indirectly sustained workplace prejudice by creating a self-centered, competitive value system.

The lack of conscious intent doesn't make workplace prejudice any less abhorrent. It does suggest, however, that regulatory reforms and awareness alone are not enough to correct the problem—as we have already witnessed.

And not all prejudice is as malicious as ethnic and gender prejudice. Not all prejudice, in fact, is unfavorable. Prejudice, as *Webster's* defines it, is "any preconceived opinion or feeling, either favorable or unfavorable."

By that definition, the workplace is replete with prejudice. And there are two primary reasons. The first has to do with the fact that decisions inevitably have to be made on limited information. Either not all the information is obtainable, or there simply isn't sufficient time to obtain it.

The second is more psychological than practical. It has to do with the need for self-affirmation, which inevitably leads to the tendency for people to see themselves, and the things that define and differentiate them, in a favorable light. People who are somehow different, as a result, may be treated differently than people who are the same.

If you are obsessed with physical fitness, for example, and pride yourself on your devotion to remaining fit and trim, you might be inclined to view your overweight and less active colleague as weak or undisciplined. It may not rise to the level of outright disgust—or even consciousness—but it can affect your ability to work together or your ability to objectively evaluate his or her work.

But before we can eliminate workplace prejudice,

or at least render it irrelevant, it's important to more fully explore what it is and where it comes from.

The Roots of Prejudice

Prejudice is an acquired thing. No one is born with it. No baby has ever come into this world with an innate dislike for anyone. Just the opposite is true. Children have an extraordinary capacity for love. Imagine how few children would love their parents if children approached love like adults do. Most parents, myself included, are undeserving of the kind of selfless, unconditional love we get from our children.

Sometimes we acquire prejudice through ignorance. Life is a process of learning, but not all learning is good. Sometimes we acquire knowledge that is inaccurate or otherwise causes us to evaluate others unfairly.

Sometimes we acquire prejudice through fear. We are naturally more inclined to judge someone unfairly if we fear that they will harm or disadvantage us in some way.

We also acquire prejudice through misunderstanding, through some form of failed communication. Somebody misunderstood somebody else or somebody said something that was misrepresented in some way.

Communication is an extremely difficult process.

That is particularly true in the workplace, where time is limited and everyone is competing for advantage. In the workplace, moreover, reward and punishment are often based on communication. Bosses form opinions about workers based on a combination of what they see, hear, and read. But the latter two forms of communication are especially vulnerable to error. "There was a miscommunication" is a common refrain in every workplace.

And as if that weren't enough to make the workplace vulnerable to prejudice, a lot of the communication that ultimately influences important processes, such as the boss's evaluation of your performance, comes from third parties, some of whom have an incentive to muck it up to your disadvantage. The boss isn't going to be able to sort out where all those little seeds of opinion in his or her head came from when it comes time to sit down and allocate raises or assign promotions. (But you don't really want the boss evaluating you in a vacuum. You want your boss to listen to what others have to say. They may have more familiarity with the quality of your work or they may correct your boss when he or she assigns unfounded blame.)

Even in the most innocent case, however, a fellow employee may unknowingly pass on information that is simply untrue. Or they may not have all the facts.

Or they may be premature or simply inaccurate in their conclusions or observations.

And then, of course, there is malicious communication—the worst kind of workplace politics. It happens for a variety of fairly complex psychological and social reasons. Sometimes it's pro-active, sometimes it's reactive.

The bottom line is that every employee's fate depends on communication that is based on limited information, takes place over a long period of time, and involves a lot of parties. It's really a surprise that the process works at all. At every turn, the door is open to mis-information and mis-judgment, not to mention manipulation, deceit, and gamesmanship.

These are the basic ingredients of prejudice. These are the things that lead to favoritism, intolerance, and injustice. In the best case, the wrong people get rewarded. In the worst cases, there is an atmosphere of distrust and a culture that promotes Machiavellian behavior.

So how do we eliminate workplace prejudice?

The Workplace Approach to Prejudice

Employees who can't get along are often advised to simply "work it out." That may stop the open warfare, at least momentarily, but it seldom solves the underlying problem. It just sweeps problems, including prejudice, under the rug.

As a solution to workplace strife, the "work it out" approach is based on the idea of tolerance. It sounds good. But it's rarely effective over the long haul.

Why? Because tolerance is a passive solution to conflict. Tolerance, as the word is commonly used today, is a form of acceptance. To really be effective, however, the conflict has to eliminated. If the problem isn't resolved, tolerance can simply drive the conflict underground.

There will always be differences of opinion, particularly among co-workers. The work of the organization is often complex and involves a whole host of variables. Co-workers are often competing with each other for advancement and income. As a result, managers—and I know because I've been one of them—frequently spend a good part of their day addressing personnel issues. There is always someone in every workplace who is finding it difficult to work with someone else. "So-and-so doesn't carry his or her load." "So-and-so is a busybody." "So-and-so can't be trusted." "So-and-so talks about me behind my back." The list is endless.

Sometimes a little extra communication can resolve

the conflict. If the conflict results from a simple misunderstanding, just getting the two parties to talk it out is often enough.

When the problem reflects some deep-seated prejudice, however, asking the participants to simply talk it out and be tolerant of each other is going to provide temporary relief only. The conflict will inevitably re-emerge.

In order to eliminate the scourge of prejudice, we need to take a more proactive approach. We need to be more than tolerant. We need to take action to eradicate prejudice and the inequitable results that it often leads to in the modern workplace.

In short, we need to substitute Christian love for passive tolerance.

The Christian Approach to Prejudice

Love isn't a word you hear bandied about the workplace very much. It's a little too "soft and fuzzy" for the gladiatorial battle that is modern business. There's an unsettling implication that love is a process that is both unpredictable and often irrational.

Webster's defines love as "a profoundly tender, passionate affection for another person, esp. when based on sexual attraction." Defined in this way, love is clearly not an appropriate emotion for the workplace. Love, by this definition, is something we possess, not live, and it is the love of modern American culture.

This "passionate affection" brand of love, however, is not the Christian love described in the Bible. Christian love is a selfless love that is lived, not possessed. And it is the key to overcoming prejudice in both the workplace and the world at large.

In Romans, we are told:

> The commandments, "Do not commit adultery," "Do not murder," "Do not steal," "Do not covet," and whatever commandment there may be, are summed up in this one rule: "Love your neighbor as yourself."
>
> ROMANS 13:9

Similarly, on the eve of his crucifixion, Jesus tells his disciples:

> A new command I give you: Love one another. As I have loved you, so you must love one another. By this all men will know that you are my disciples, if you love one another.
>
> JOHN 13:34-35

Strong's Exhaustive Concordance lists more than five-hundred references to love or its variants. No other single concept, with the exception of the need to act, which is often applied to the concept of love, gets as much biblical attention or prominence.

But what, exactly, is Christian love?

Christian love is not an "instant fix" but rather a journey that begins with faith and is followed by goodness, knowledge, self-control, perseverance, godliness, and brotherly kindness, and it culminates in love. Consider this passage from the Second Book of Peter:

> Make every effort to add to your faith goodness; and to goodness, knowledge; and to knowledge, self-control; and to self-control, perseverance; and to perseverance, godliness; and to godliness, brotherly kindness; and to brotherly kindness, love.
>
> 2 PETER 1:5–7

It seems clear that these qualities are cumulative. We must, in other words, acquire one quality before we can acquire the next, creating, if you will, a hierarchy of Christian character qualities, with love at the top.

This has many implications, not the least of which is that love is not something that just appears randomly and without apparent reason. Christian love is developed in a methodical, step-by-step process. It is not something that we possess, like a car or a job title.

It is not something that we "fall into" or are smitten by. It is nothing less than that which defines us as Christians. Let's take a closer look.

The Building Blocks of Love

According to Peter, the first building block is *faith*. Without faith, nothing else really matters, for without faith we can have no life view. If we just live and we die, then life has no purpose. It just happens. If we have faith, however, our life has purpose, and we will seek to understand what that purpose is. Faith, therefore, is the launching pad of spiritual exploration. If we have faith, we are not content to be spiritually at rest. Our spiritual curiosity inevitably gets the best of us, and we begin our spiritual journey.

The second building block is *goodness*, or virtue. Virtuous living is easy to understand but difficult to achieve. The Bible spells out how God wants us to live in pretty clear detail. It's also pretty clear, however, that we won't live this virtuous life without God's help. That, of course, is by design. God is nudging us to reach out, to claim God's freely offered love.

Having sought goodness, we are then ready to acquire *knowledge*, the third building block. God doesn't want a relationship of blind obedience. If obedience is all that God cares about, surely our obedience could be forced. God, however, doesn't want us to simply go through the motions of spirituality, adhering to the rules without understanding them. God wants us to *choose* to know God, not to abandon ourselves out of fear or to the expectation of a simple *quid pro quo* (i.e., we obey the rules and we go to heaven). To know God in such an intimate and active sense, we need to delve deeper and deeper into what God wants us to learn. We need to strive to understand God's word so that we can make a conscious choice to accept it and adopt it.

A choice is valid, however, only as long as we follow through on it. That's where *self-control*, the fourth building block, comes in. It's not enough to have Christian knowledge. We must live it. Passive acceptance is not enough. We must act upon it.

At times, of course, our self-control will fail. That's why we need *perseverance*, the fifth building block. Our Christian journey is a journey of exploration, understanding, and re-affirmation. Will power alone is not enough. Staying the Christian course requires the discipline of recurring choice. Perseverance is essential, for we know that our commitment will inevitably be challenged by life events.

If we persevere, we will develop an increasing awe and reverence for God. This is what Peter refers to as *godliness*, the sixth building block.

Out of our deep connection with God, we can

develop connections to the people around us. We will see and understand our shared and equal place in God's earthly world and eternal kingdom. We will experience a sense of connection and sharing, which Peter calls *brotherly kindness*, that transcends simple empathy.

Finally, once we have acquired faith and have developed the qualities of virtue, knowledge, self-control, perseverance, godliness, and brotherly kindness, we are ready to love. This is a love that is filled with trust, respect, and understanding that far exceeds civility or tolerance. This is a love that allows us to reach out to our enemies and forgive those who persecute us. This is a love that can nullify the presumptions and ignorance that are at the heart of prejudice.

In short, this is a love that cannot co-exist with prejudice. This is a love that will allow us to forgive those who victimize us with prejudice in the workplace. This is a love that will take us to a higher ground. This is the only kind of love that can eradicate prejudice.

Love at Work

Whether we are the victim or the victimizer, our understanding and adoption of the concept of Christian love can re-shape the workplace. Consider this passage from 1 Corinthians:

> Love is patient, love is kind. It does not envy,
> it does not boast, it is not proud. It is not rude,
> it is not self-seeking, it is not easily angered,
> it keeps no record of wrongs. Love does not
> delight in evil but rejoices with the truth. It
> always protects, always trusts, always hopes,
> always perseveres. . . . And now these three
> remain: faith, hope and love. But the greatest
> of these is love.
>
> 1 Corinthians 13:4–7, 13

Christian love is unqualified. It rises above all else. No earthly strife or conflict can ultimately overpower it. Love will always prevail.

Workplace prejudice is no exception. It cannot exist in the presence of Christian love. To the extent that we seek to develop the building blocks of Christian character that are essential to Christian love, we can neither be purveyors nor victims of prejudice.

Said differently, in all of the cases of workplace strife that I have been asked to referee as a manager or supervisor, I can't recall a single one where the antagonists were making any attempt whatsoever to move up the Christian hierarchy of character as described by Peter. In each and every case, the individuals involved were thinking of themselves and were motivated by secular goals of competition and self-promotion.

On the flip side, the people whom I have witnessed enjoying the most respect in the workplace were those who best embodied the principles of Christian love. They lived and worked by very strong principles of morality, fairness, humility, and self-sacrifice. They lived by the Christian building blocks outlined by Peter.

Inevitably, these individuals changed the workplace around them for the better, not through manipulation and political maneuvering, but by their example. The reason is simple: We all want a life purpose, and the self-esteem and validation that go with it. And these are the people who have it. These are the people we want to emulate.

My own father was a man of very strong principles, and no one ever said that he was a man without an opinion. But he wasn't perfect. He would have been the last person to ever suggest he was.

Sadly, he was taken at the young age of forty-nine by cancer after a long, difficult battle with this dreadful disease. Some years later, however, I had the opportunity to work with several people who had worked with him, and I was pleasantly amazed at how uniformly revered he had been as a boss and co-worker. Everyone loved him.

Not one of those individuals, however, praised my father for his tolerance or suggested that he had an "anything goes" attitude that they greatly admired.

Each and every one of them praised him as a man of principles, a man who believed in the right things and who stood steadfastly by those beliefs. In short, everyone admired him because he was a man of goodness, knowledge, self-control, perseverance, godliness, and brotherly kindness, which, in turn, caused them to love him in the most flattering way possible.

Christian love is something we need to work at, to strive for. Rather than being a state of mind or a state of passionate affection, Christian love is a way to *live*. That's what ultimately makes Christian love such a powerful force. It is not professed. Rather, it is built through deeds of kindness and service.

And deeds are far more powerful than communication in eliminating the kind of ignorance or false preconception that prejudice is typically built upon. Deeds have more clarity than words. They are less open to interpretation or manipulation. They have a permanence that simple communication often lacks.

In the end, it doesn't matter that there's someone in your workplace who doesn't like you or who wakes up every morning thinking of ways to annoy you. It doesn't matter that you are forced to work with a sexist or a bigot. It doesn't matter that workplace politics define your workplace culture.

You can push all of this into irrelevancy by developing your Christian character and practicing your ability to love. This is not to say, of course, that prejudice should be overlooked or tolerated. Acquiescence isn't the answer. If, however, you devote yourself to building Christian character and practicing Christian love, you will not be accepting prejudice, but overcoming it. You will be eradicating the ignorance, fear, and misunderstanding that are the very core of prejudice.

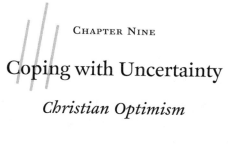

CHAPTER NINE

Coping with Uncertainty

Christian Optimism

Do you work under a cloud of uncertainty? Are you fearful of the future?

I once worked with an executive who kept a sign on the front of his desk that read "No Surprises." He meant, of course, no *bad* surprises.

Unfortunately, the workplace has become significantly less predictable at a time when the cost of failure has risen dramatically. Few employees have any meaningful margin for error in their work. You may no longer have the luxury of learning from your mistakes or growing into the job.

In fact, there's no such thing as "*having* a job" anymore. You may receive a paycheck, but you don't have any guarantee that those paychecks will continue to come. Don't think for a minute that you can't be one of the statistics.

I know. I've been there. I lost my job in the late

1990s, at the height of what had been, until then, a very successful career.

Cracks in the System

I never thought I would lose my job. I *lived* my work. I threw everything I had into it. I carried it with me 24/7. But in the time it took to have a short conversation with my boss, I was left with nothing to carry.

It's hard not to worry about the future. Uncertainty abounds. Pick up any business magazine—or any magazine, for that matter—and virtually all you'll read about is change. No business leader or social forecaster would dare suggest that the future will look a lot like the past.

But change alone doesn't explain the uncertainty that hangs over the modern workplace. In reality, change has been a constant since the beginning of time. There's something more at work, and we need to take a minute to understand what that "something more" is.

Employment law is largely governed by the doctrine of employment-at-will, which came out of an 1877 legal treatise by Horace Wood entitled "Master and Servant." While the legal justification has long been debated, it appears to be a *quid pro quo* arrangement. If employees were prohibited from quitting, they would essentially be indentured servants. And if employees could quit whenever they wanted, shouldn't an employer have the right to fire employees whenever it chose as well?

In recent decades, however, legislatures have been constricting this employment-at-will doctrine, putting more and more restrictions on employers in an attempt to eliminate prejudicial discrimination. Minority, female, and older workers are now considered "protected classes" in the workplace. The effectiveness of these workplace protection laws, however, is less than clear. Members of all protected classes, as well as members of the non-protected classes, continue to lose their jobs in substantial numbers.

When I started my career, there was an implied contract between employer and employee which held that if the employee worked hard, remained loyal, and did his or her best, the employer would do everything possible to keep that employee on the payroll. Frankly, it never occurred to me or my co-workers that we could be fired for an honest mistake or simply to increase company earnings. It just wasn't done.

Cracks started to appear in this implied *quid pro quo* arrangement in the 1970s, in response to the perceived economic threat of Japan Inc., which was transforming the global competitive landscape. In response, American businesses began to view their employees more as an expense than an asset. There was almost a unilateral retraction of the implied employment "contract." If profits fell, jobs would be cut.

A Culture of Pessimism

There are few places where we'll encounter more anxiety and hand-wringing about the future than on the job. And the abolition of job security is only part of the explanation.

The workplace lives by the complementary processes of planning and control. Companies of every size and stripe operate by the same basic processes: They plan for a future they find acceptable and then marshal their organizational energy to create that future.

Big companies, in particular, spend incalculable hours and resources planning, re-planning, and re-planning again. Numbers are incessantly poured into computer models and spreadsheets designed to simulate future outcomes. Projects are scheduled in infinite detail. And tasks are assigned with deadlines by which to measure progress and performance.

Once the plan is in place, the company turns its attention to ensuring its prophecy. Reams of paper are consumed by tally sheets, progress reports, and status updates. The company motivates itself to realize its plans through a combination of inspiration and accountability. With carrots and sticks, the company incentivizes its employees with the promise of financial reward and advancement for meeting or exceeding expectations while threatening punishment for falling short.

The Achilles heel of planning and control is unexpected change. Things don't always work out as we expect them to. Today, in fact, they seldom do. There are just too many variables to know with certainty how events will unfold.

The workplace takes a variety of approaches to this uncertainty. Some companies rely on draconian accountability in their attempt to bend future reality to their will. Others rely on being agile and nimble enough to react to unexpected change. A few rely on the personal vision of their leader. And still others seek to minimize the surprises through exhaustive study and research.

In each case, however, there is a fundamental assumption that the future will look like the past—or that change will at least be predictable. In our modern world of rapid change, unfortunately, this is an increasingly poor assumption.

There is a further underlying assumption of pessimism. Companies assume that, left to its own, the future is a world of failure. If they don't make their own success, in other words, they won't have any.

This is a pretty cynical view of the world. It's hard

to find hope in a culture that doesn't believe in hope. It's hard to be upbeat in an environment where much of what goes on is predicated on the near inevitability of failure.

The workplace culture, as a result, is typically a very cautious one. While there is a professed recognition of the need to take risks and embrace change, most companies are risk averse. Working in such an environment day in and day out, we inevitably adopt the workplace perspective as our own. We become suspicious and practice caution. We assume the worst when confronted with new circumstances. In other words, we mirror the workplace pessimism.

In fairness, however, the workplace is not solely responsible for our predilection to view the glass as half-empty. Modern communication, as wonderful as it is in many respects, doesn't help. If anything truly unfortunate happens, we're sure to hear about it. The seed of perceived risk is unavoidably planted, naturally reinforcing our caution.

In April 2003, for example, I had to attend a business meeting in Toronto. It was at the height of the SARS epidemic, which was obviously a tragic event for the people who were affected by the disease. Judging from the reporting of the American media, however, I expected to arrive to a sea of surgical masks and the cacophonous blare of ambulance sirens. I was admittedly anxious and wondered if I was putting a business meeting ahead of the interests of my family. I seriously considered canceling, even though it was an important meeting and others were relying on my attendance.

I was staying at a large hotel downtown, which, on prior stays, had always been bustling with people and activity. This time, however, the lobby was empty. While the hotel had been virtually sold out for the evening just a few weeks earlier, I was told, cancellations had brought the occupancy rate down to thirty percent.

When I went out to dinner that night, my experience was much the same. The hostess at the large restaurant where I ate said that, while the restaurant would normally be full most evenings, there had been only one couple dining the night before.

And yet, during my two-day stay, I didn't see a single surgical mask or hear a single siren. I didn't talk to a single person who personally knew anyone who had contracted the disease. Not one. Other than the empty hotel and restaurants, and the virtual absence of public taxi cabs—which the few visitors there were avoiding out of fear of contamination—my visit was the same as all of my other visits to this wonderful city.

Ironically, science, too, has contributed to modern-day caution and skepticism. While science can help us to understand what is possible, it also extends our perceived understanding of what *isn't* possible. We know, for example, that water cannot flow uphill, that two plus two can never equal five. And if our understanding presupposes a future reality that resembles the current reality, what we know may be more limiting than helpful.

That's exactly what led Thomas Watson, the chairman of IBM, to state in 1943, "I think there is a world market for maybe five computers." And why Decca Recording Company, in 1962, rejected the Beatles with the comment, "We don't like their sound, and guitar music is on the way out." Even Albert Einstein couldn't predict the future with accuracy. He proclaimed, "There is not the slightest indication that nuclear energy will ever be obtainable. It would mean that the atom would have to be shattered at will."

In each case, these predictions were made by informed people and were in line with what was known at the time. Each was an accurate extrapolation of then-current realities. As it turned out, however, the future looked nothing like those realities or the predictions that flowed from them.

The future will be a very different place than we are accustomed to. Surprises will come from unexpected sources. Unpredicted change will be the rule rather than the exception. All of this combines to reduce our sense of personal security and dampens our historical comfort that hard work will pay off.

It's no wonder we're worried. It would be unnatural not to be. A healthy amount of skepticism is clearly warranted. It's a fine line, however, between healthy doubt and toxic fear. When our doubt overwhelms us, we may retreat from the world around us or panic our way into self-destructive behaviors. Either way, our doubt becomes a burden to our health and our happiness.

There is, thankfully, a way to move beyond this culture of pessimism.

A Culture of Possibility

In the book of Genesis, there is a heartening story that begins with Abraham sitting at the entrance to his tent during the heat of the day. He looked up to see three men standing nearby, one of whom turned out to be God (although scholars seem to disagree as to when Abraham realized this).

At any rate, as was the custom of the day, Abraham was very hospitable to the three strangers. He invited them to sit in the shade of a nearby tree and rest. He brought them water and rushed inside to tell his wife, Sarah, to bake some fresh bread. Then he rushed off to his herd to prepare a choice calf for his guests.

After the feast was presented, one of the three

strangers asked as to the whereabouts of Sarah. After learning that she was inside the tent, the stranger announced that Sarah would have a son by the next time he returned.

While Abraham and Sarah desperately wanted a son, Sarah was well past the age of childbearing. Understandably , she was skeptical.

God was aware of Sarah's reaction and chastised her for her doubt, pointing out that anything was within God's ability, and promising again that she would be with child within a year. And, as it turned out, she was, with a son that became the first in a long line of kings.

At the time, however, Sarah's line of reasoning was based on deductive logic, that is, what she could deduct from observable facts. But deductive logic is naturally backward-looking and, as an approach to the future, is self-limiting. It precludes the leap of faith.

What God was offering was a future based on possibility. God was asking Sarah to defy conventional wisdom, to believe that her long-held dream could come true.

That's exactly what James "Doc" Counsilman did, when, at the age of 58, he successfully swam the English Channel. Or what Yuichiro Miura did, when, at the age of 70, he successfully ascended Mt. Everest.

Or what Corwin Peterson did, when, at the spry age of 68, he successfully trekked to the North Pole *on foot*.

At the age of 70, Prussian-born English evangelist and philanthropist, George Müller (1805–1898), began a seventeen-year series of missionary and evangelistic tours that took him over 200,000 miles and allowed him to preach to some three million people. At the age of 60, Jesse Irvin Overholtzer founded the Child Evangelism Fellowship (CEF) ministry. Sixty-five years later, CEF now has 1,200 missionaries overseas, 700 full-time workers in the United States and Canada, and some 40,000 volunteers serving the ministry. And Clara McBride Hale, at the age of 63, took in the baby of a drunken mother she didn't know, and then went on to found The Hale House for addicted children 15 years later.

Each of these people rejected the world of pessimism and embraced the possibility of the future. Each of them looked forward with hope and optimism.

Skepticism is limiting; despair is debilitating. But optimism is an enabler. The future always holds promise if we have the faith to be open to it.

I'm not suggesting a blind faith. You probably won't fare well if you go into your next project review meeting and suggest that there's no need to worry because God will take care of everything. You can, however, differentiate between the institutional pessimism that defines the workplace culture and the optimism of faith that can define your personal behavior. There will be disappointment and failure. You can't change that. But so, too, can there be great and unexpected reward. If you aren't limited by pessimism, the possibilities are endless.

Yes, I can hear you arguing, "That's a whole lot easier said than done." And you are absolutely correct. But the good news is that we're not called to this faith alone.

Trusting God for the Future

When I lost my job, the world as I knew it came to an end. I wondered how we would pay the bills. I told myself and my wife at least a dozen times that the money had run out and we could no longer meet our obligations. But somehow we always did. In some cases, the money arrived miraculously—in the most literal sense. In others, opportunities arose just as the last grain of sand was falling through the neck of the hourglass.

It took some creative juggling for our family to get by with one car for a while. (I live in a suburb of The Motor City, so there's virtually no mass transit.) It took us some time to work out scheduling, and both my wife and I found ourselves, on more than a few occasions, heading for the garage to go somewhere only to discover that the garage was empty. Sometimes we had to borrow a car. Sometimes we rented one. Sometimes we just had to wait. Eventually, however, we got to where we needed to go. We got through the financial hardship, and we both learned that life goes on.

It began to dawn on me, during this period, that the real fear of job loss is not financial, but personal: I had lost my personal identity. Prior to my termination, I had defined myself largely by the job I held, by the title I had been granted, by the "success" I had achieved. That identity, I ultimately had to accept, was gone forever. I would never get it back.

There were moments when I wondered how my two young daughters could ever be proud of me again. There were moments when I wondered how my wife could ever love and respect me. These were feelings I had never experienced before. These were the fears that filled my days and nights.

For many people, including myself, however, job loss turns out to be a great life opportunity, a time of deep reflection and soul searching. Many of us have discovered that we weren't doing what we really wanted to do. We thought we enjoyed our work, but we were really just riding it out because that was the safest and most comfortable thing to do.

Losing my job was one of the most stressful events

I've had to endure. Yet I found strength from three
sources: a supportive, loving spouse; nonjudgmental
family and friends; and the Bible. In particular, the
following passage from the book of Matthew helped
me get through this very trying period:

> Therefore I tell you, do not worry about your
> life, what you will eat or drink; or about your
> body, what you will wear. Is not life more im-
> portant than food, and the body more impor-
> tant than clothes? Look at the birds of the air;
> they do not sow or reap or store away in barns,
> and yet your heavenly Father feeds them. Are
> you not much more valuable than they? Who
> of you by worrying can add a single hour to his
> life?
>
> And why do you worry about clothes? See
> how the lilies of the field grow. They do not
> labor or spin. Yet I tell you that not even Solo-
> mon in all his splendor was dressed like one
> of these. If that is how God clothes the grass
> of the field, which is here today and tomor-
> row is thrown into the fire, will he not much
> more clothe you, O you of little faith? So do not
> worry, saying, "What shall we eat?" or "What
> shall we drink?" or "What shall we wear?" For

the pagans run after all these things, and your heavenly Father knows that you need them. But seek first his kingdom and his righteousness, and all these things will be given to you as well. Therefore do not worry about tomorrow, for tomorrow will worry about itself. Each day has enough trouble of its own.

MATTHEW 6:25–34

"Do not worry about your life." That's pretty reassuring, don't you think?

I'd be dishonest if I suggested that I never get down or never worry about money. I do. But when I do, I think about this passage. I go for a walk and look at the flowers and the birds. I look at the lake or the river or the trickling stream. I look at the green meadow or the snow-covered mountain or the fog as it rolls down the valley. And when I do, I am reassured once again that God knows what I need and will provide it.

Most importantly, I know that how I make my living will never make me as important as any of these things. A fancy title will never make me as awe-inspiring as a mountain. An attractive office will never give me the beauty of a field of flowers. All of the accomplishments I make will never make me as radiant as the smile of a sunflower.

Did you know that the word "hope" used to mean trust or confidence? It did. It's now an archaic use of the word, but I, for one, would like to bring it back. Hope without trust is merely desire. But when we put our trust in God, we have hope for the future, based on the confidence that God is with us.

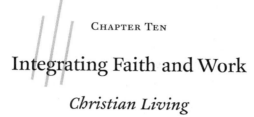

CHAPTER TEN

Integrating Faith and Work

Christian Living

We've explored how to deal with the stress and anxiety of the modern workplace through the pursuit of Christian ideals, such as courage and perseverance. But what actions can we take to actually put these ideals to work on the job?

In the end, it comes down to this: Believe and act. I propose that this takes place in three ways: Live to serve, live to know, and live to grow.

Live to Serve

There are numerous stories throughout the Bible about the importance of service to others. Jesus, it has been said many times, was the ultimate servant leader. On the night before his death, he literally washed the feet of his disciples, saying, "Unless I wash you, you have no part with me" (John 13:8). Everything Jesus did, he did for the glory of God: "If I glorify myself, my glory means nothing. My Father . . . is the one who glorifies me" (John 8:54).

We often think of service to others in terms of sacrifice. As a result, we view the process of service with a "half-empty" perspective. We think of it as an "exchange," a process akin to what mathematicians refer to as a zero-sum game, by which they mean that one participant has to lose for the other to gain.

Is that how you think of your work? Do you think of your job as a *quid pro quo* arrangement where your knowledge and your skills are exchanged for the currency you need to turn your work into the goods and services you want and need?

In fact, that's exactly how the modern employer/employee relationship is structured. It is designed to be a commercial exchange of your labor for the company's money.

That sounds reasonable, doesn't it? And it is—if our only objective in life is to survive. The current arrangement is probably sufficient if all we want is to put food on the table and a roof over our heads. By this definition, however, work is nothing more than a break-even proposition.

Consider this: You spend something close to half of your waking hours on the job. Do you really want to spend that much of your active life on a break-even proposition?

I don't. And I doubt you do either. But what if we adopted a different perspective? What if we unilaterally threw out the *quid pro quo* arrangement and declared that we would live—*and work*—as Jesus did, in service of others, for the glory of God? That we would honor God through our work. That we would be God's servants through our work. Then even the most mundane, tedious tasks would take on an entirely different meaning.

Do you enjoy puttering around the house? I do. I've tried golf; it's too frustrating. What I'd rather do on a Saturday morning is mow the lawn or edge the flower beds. It's not that I have anything against golf or any other form of recreation. It's just not for me. I get more out of doing my chores than I would spending the day trying to find a little white ball among the trees and bushes. It's just the way I'm wired.

Actually, I think it's largely a reflection of how I was raised. I recall moving into a new house when I was about ten years old. My older brother and I, at our father's behest, were out mowing the lawn one weekend, using one of those old non-motorized push mowers.

Seeing us struggling to push this mechanical beast around the lawn, the lady next door (her husband was playing golf) came over to offer my father the use of their power mower. To this my father replied,

"I appreciate your kind offer, but I already have *two* power mowers, and they work just fine."

My father taught me more than the value of hard work, however. If that had been the full extent of it, I'd probably hate working around the house today. What he taught me, more importantly, was the dignity of all work.

I remember a New York City taxicab driver who drove me from La Guardia airport to Manhattan. He was very friendly and talkative, and soon began telling me the story of his life. He had emigrated to the United States with his wife and two young sons some years before, showing up with his clothes and not much else.

In the time he had been in the United States, however, working only as a cab driver, he had put both of his sons through college *and* graduate school. One son had earned a Ph.D. from M.I.T. and the other graduated from the Stanford Medical School. He was so proud that he pulled over to the side of the road, turned off the meter, and produced his sons' college identification cards for me to see. His commitment was both inspiring and contagious. For him, driving a cab was not about earning tips and fares; it was all about creating a bright future for his sons.

One summer during my college years, I worked in a factory. One day my boss asked me to take one of the trucks and deliver a load of cartons to a nearby organization that provided jobs for special needs adults. It seems that someone in the factory had forgotten to insert some paperwork into the cartons before sealing them. Rather than sending them back to the factory to be re-opened, my employer hired this organization to do it instead.

It was obviously a very simple job, as boring as could be. So, as a young man of nineteen, I was literally stunned to see how much pride these special people took in their simple task. It was truly inspiring. When they helped me to load or unload the truck, my biggest challenge—beyond overcoming my guilt for not being so appreciative of my many blessings—was curbing their enthusiasm so they wouldn't get hurt.

In each of these cases, people chose to see their jobs as something more than a *quid pro quo* arrangement. They, in the most literal sense, were working for something greater than themselves. No matter how others might have judged the importance of their work, they chose to see their work in the broader perspective of service.

It's a valuable perspective no matter what you do at what level of the organization. All of the money and all of the status in the world will not give you personal fulfillment. I know. I lived the experience. I lived in a big house and drove a fancy car and vacationed in exotic places. I commanded the respect and deference of total strangers in response to my fancy title and my perceived social status. And I had a hole in my heart that made it difficult to get out of bed in the morning.

We each need to find that deeper, broader meaning in our work. We need to see our work as more than doing what we're told, or what is expected. We need to know that what we are doing has more value than a paycheck. And we can do that by bringing God into our work.

It doesn't matter how religion-averse your workplace is. You don't have to violate a single workplace rule. You don't have to offend your co-workers or annoy the boss. All you have to do is change your perspective. When you choose to work with dignity, gratitude, and commitment, your work honors God. When you live to serve, you will have what is most valuable.

Live to Know

Sometimes it difficult to know what's a blessing and what isn't. Sometimes misfortune, even tragedy, is a blessing in disguise.

When I was eight years old, I started to have seizures that sent me crashing to the ground. Eventually the seizures became so severe and so frequent that I could not attend school. I even had to wear protective head gear at all times.

I was ultimately admitted to a large metropolitan children's hospital that had an entire ward devoted to seizure disorders. I was put in a large, open room with about twenty-five other kids, our metal beds lined up side-by-side along the two longest walls of the narrow ward.

I was frightened. I didn't understand. I felt isolated. I felt different.

About a year after the seizures began, the doctors were running an excruciatingly painful diagnostic procedure known as a pneumoencephalogram. It involves inserting a large needle into the spinal chord—without the benefit of general anesthesia—and removing the cerebrospinal fluid from around the brain and replacing it with oxygen, allowing for a more vivid and detailed x-ray of the brain.

Because it was strictly a diagnostic procedure, you can imagine the doctors' surprise when it completely cured me. To this day, I haven't had another seizure. And they still don't know why, although they speculate that a virus was living against the fibrous membrane that lines the inside of the skull. Removing the cerebrospinal fluid, they speculate, deprived the virus of its life support, and it died off.

My parents, of course, were ecstatic. As was I. The experience taught me some very valuable lessons and helped to shape the person that I am today. First and foremost, I learned what it meant to be different. The compassion that I acquired among the children of that ward played a large role in defining how I would live and work as an adult. God was surely creating blessings in the midst of those turbulent times. I just didn't know it.

Whenever anything happens to me—good or bad—I remind myself now to consider how God might be working in my life and to what purpose. How is this event, or these circumstances, moving me toward becoming the person God intends me to be? I think of it as *living to know*.

The fact that God is constantly working in our lives is not always immediately obvious, especially when we're caught up in a hectic work day. But if we seek to know, I think there are numerous ways in which we can keep ourselves open to God's possibility—even at work.

I personally carry on an ongoing dialogue with God. Sometimes it's a simple, fleeting thought. At other times, it's more of an extended dialogue. I talk to God when I'm alone in the car or waiting for an appointment. I ponder God when I eat lunch or am waiting in line. Communicating with God is simply an integral part of every list of things to do.

Living to know is an exciting way to approach the work day. It will help you shed the everyday angers and disappointments that bring stress. It will help you view your life, as it unfolds, in a more positive way. And it will constantly bring you closer to God.

Live to Grow

If there is one final thought I want to leave you with, it is this: Live to grow. By that, I mean get up every morning and tell yourself that you want to end the day in a spiritually better place than when you started it.

I'm not suggesting this as a burden to take on requiring more work. I'm talking about having an attitude about the day that is expectant, open to seeing what God will do. Working in a way that glorifies God. Having a mind-set of service. Having the perspective that God is continually acting in your life.

This might take shape in any number of ways. Tape a scripture quote to the inside of your day planner or to the cover of your PDA. Read the Bible over your morning coffee. Reach out to others. Start a conversation with someone who struggles with shyness or is shunned by the rest of the workgroup. Show humility.

Be kind. Do a good job. Praise others when they do a good job.

In other words, take God to work. *Live* your faith there. And always, hold onto God's promise to be with you:

> I will guide [you].
> I will turn darkness into light before [you]
> and make the rough places smooth.
>
> Isaiah 42:16

Acknowledgments

Before I wrote my first book, I often wondered why authors bothered with acknowledgments. Who, after all, actually reads them?

I now realize, however, that authors write acknowledgments because authors don't write books alone. Books are written by a rather extended family of individuals, all of whom play an important role.

For starters, I am deeply indebted to Peg Sanders, who happens to be my mother-in-law. She is a retired high school English teacher and one of the few people I know who can still diagram a sentence. Through her limitless patience, I finally learned what I should have learned in high school English class more than thirty years ago.

Good grammar alone, however, does not make a book good. That takes the guidance of a skilled editor. In this case, I worked with the best, Marcia Broucek. If this book enjoys any success, she will deserve a large amount of the credit.

I'd also like to thank all of the people at Cowley Publications for their tireless effort and professionalism. I'd particularly like to thank Michael Wilt, editorial director, who was the first to see the possibilities for this project and whose confidence in me will forever be appreciated.

To my friends and family, I am deeply indebted for your unfailing support and constant encouragement. I'd particularly like to thank my friend Steve Merrill, who is a constant source of great inspiration and fortification; my mother, Patricia Moreau-Pickard, who has always believed in me, even when I didn't deserve it; my wife, Charlotte, without whom this wonderful journey would never have been possible; and my daughters, Leah and Ava, in whose eyes I witness God's presence each and every day.

I'd like to thank my Christian family at the Kensington Community Church in Troy, Michigan, both for their guidance and their warm embrace. I'd particularly like to thank Dave Nelson, now the lead pastor at K2, The Church, in Salt Lake City, for jumping out of an airplane and finally convincing me to let go in the name of God. And to my fellow workers in the Treasure Island children's program, who are some of the most selfless and caring people I have ever had the pleasure to know, I give thanks for your example and your fellowship.

And last, but certainly not least, I would like to thank God. Please, O Lord, help me to be worthy of your boundless love.